Paula Pryke's Flower School

Paula Pryke's Flower School

Mastering the Art of Floral Design

Photography   Sian Irvine

RIZZOLI
NEW YORK

This book is dedicated to all the people who have attended our flower classes in the United Kingdom or been present at one of my many overseas or home demonstrations. Many have become regular visitors making our flower school in London feel more of a club than a school. Several have gone onto become firm friends, and in particular I would like to dedicate this book to my very dear flower soul mate Sybil Sylvester! Long may the magic of flowers continue to inspire and beguile us all!

First published in the United States of America in 2006 by Rizzoli International Publications, Inc. 300 Park Avenue South, New York, NY 10010 www.rizzoliusa.com

© Jacqui Small LLP 2006
An imprint of Aurum Press Ltd,
25 Bedford Avenue, London WC1B 3AT

Publisher Jacqui Small
Editorial Manager Kate John
Editor Sian Parkhouse
Designer Maggie Town
Production Peter Colley

ISBN-10: 0-8478-2805-0
ISBN-13: 978-0-8478-2805-0

Library of Congress Control Number 2005907112

Second printing, March 2007
2007   2008   2009
10 9 8 7 6 5 4 3 2

Printed and bound in China

contents

introduction

Everything you need to know to arrange flowers in the Paula Pryke style can be found in this book, whether you wish to be a competent flower arranger or whether you are the serious student of floristry. Once you have learned the basics—the techniques and the elements of good floral design—you will be able to create any design you wish. When you have mastered these skills, you can start to create your own style and in time become a serious floral artist. Designing with flowers has given me immense pleasure over many years, and I feel very grateful to have found this vocation. Above all, I hope that this book will spread the gospel: good floral design is enjoyable and rewarding for everyone—not least the floral designer!

Contemporary floristry has developed enormously over the last four decades, and new styles are constantly emerging and gaining prominence. The industry is becoming a much more integral part of modern design and is led by architecture, art, interior design, and fashion. Within each of the main continents there are distinct styles and influences, and for the last thirty years it would seem that Europe has been the major focus of attention for new styles. One of the main reasons why the standard has been so high in continental Europe is that generally there has been a greater regard for the importance of professional training. Generally this means that before someone opens a floristry business, they have had some formal training and apprenticeship. It is far more common in Europe to find that a florist is an accredited Master florist who has learned his or her craft as a full-time student of floristry and has served some apprenticeship with another professional before starting their own business. In these European countries, you are far less likely to have anyone start a flower shop and call him or herself a "Designer Florist!" without any formal training because the competition is so strong. At the moment anyone can start a flower business in the United

Kingdom and in some other parts of the world such as the United States, and it is relatively easy to set up business. Lots of people have a very romantic view of the flower industry and think that working with flowers will be the panacea for life. They set up a business before they have fully mastered the basic skills or at worst are not even aware that they have huge gaps in their floristry and business knowledge. I have to confess that I changed careers and "fast-tracked" my study of floristry. At the time, I was "lucky" that the flower industry in London was not very developed and lacked any media profile. My fresh approach to flower arranging and the artistic way the shop was laid out immediately attracted many clients and the media's interest. At the same time several other designers opened shops and businesses in London, and before long we were all competing for work in the same marketplace. This pushed up the standard of floristry, and now in hindsight I can see I was at the start of this revolution in floristry in Britain. At the time I was too busy working and trying to make the business profitable to notice!

Northern continental Europe has also produced some very impressive florists, particularly from Sweden,

Denmark, Norway, Austria, and Switzerland. The style of German floristry has always been very strong, and certain florists, such as Gregor Lersch, have tirelessly spread unique talents throughout the world by lecturing and demonstrating worldwide as well as teaching in his native Germany at his base in Bad Neuenahr. As the Netherlands has such supremacy in the world flower market, it is not very surprising to discover that they, too, have many fine florists and have been very prominent in moving forward the professionalism of the flower industry. The Flower Council of Holland has helped to promote good design as well as flower marketing. Marcel Wolterick is my favorite Dutch contemporary, whose sumptuous designs make the most of the individual flowers. Belgium has spawned some very talented florists, with Daniel Ost being the most well known internationally. The style for the Belgians and French is generally more romantic and flowery than in the more northern parts of Europe, and one of my favorite florists is Christian Tortu, whose natural, fresh style always delights me. Many of these talented people, through increased

international travel and the new media, have impacted on floristry style worldwide. Emerging interest in floristry is now coming from China, Vietnam, and Thailand as well as lots of South American countries. There is also an interesting merge of Eastern and Western floral design, with the strong influence of ikebana permeating European design and many Japanese students moving from ikebana to European design.

In the UK, we have always had a deep interest and passion in gardening, and this spawned "florists" who worked initially with the big houses and their lavish gardens and later in the "custom" nurseries. The occupational florist and flower shopkeeper emerged in the twentieth century. Floristry is the term given to the world of the professional florist who earns a living from working with the natural plant world. Flower arranging was the domain of the lady at home who was usually an amateur and who enjoyed arranging flowers either for the church or in flower clubs. Very often these amateur flower arrangers would join a club and exhibit or compete with other flower arrangers. The garden was an important source of plant material, and generally they had no commercial side to their hobby. Over the past ten years, this distinction has blurred, and more people are turning a hobby into a business at the same time that there is more commercial interest in the flower industry. Department stores, supermarkets, and gas stations are selling flowers, and internet companies sell direct from the growers. More and more flowers are being sold on British street vendors by market stalls, and the variety of people involved with the flower industry has mushroomed enormously.

I started my own floristry career by training at the famous Constance Spry School for floristry. I then went on to study in a traditional, professional floristry course at a vocational college in London and worked as an apprentice to a London florist. I immersed myself in floristry and flowers and devoured every book I could find on the subject. I visited many shops to access the marketplace, and wholesalers and garden centers to broaden my knowledge. After three years of working part-time in a flower shop and cramming myself with information, I took the plunge and rather naively opened my own flower shop. My fresh and natural new style hit London at a time when British floristry was sadly lacking in flair. However, within a few years of opening my shop, there emerged a group of new floral designers, many of whom, like myself, had come from other career directions, and soon we were competing for work and raising the standard of floristry first in the capital and then throughout the United Kingdom. Just three years after I began my business, I was approached to write my first book, and it was at this point that I realized that I had established a unique new style of floral design.

Paula Pryke

I feel strongly that the role of a florist is to interpret artistically the ideas and requests of his or her clients with plant material. At one level this could be a hugely creative art form, making giant decorative structures that command an immense budget for plant material, or at completely the other end of the spectrum—but no less worthy— creating a simple tied bunch of flowers as a "thank you" gesture, or artistically wrapping a simple stem as a tribute for a memorial service. It is only occasionally that we have the opportunity to be completely and unrestrainedly creative and innovative and design solely for our own satisfaction. This may be in our own homes, for a competition, or when we are working on new collections of personal floristry work. Whether designing for ourselves or for others, over a period of time we create our own style.

my signature style

Massed monochromatic flowers are a favorite of mine, not least since massing is one design style that looks very effective both in informal and formal situations. I most often use all one type of massed flower or monochromatic arrangements in my own home where the strength of color in the arrangement highlights a room. The use of one color throughout a party theme or decorating an event creates a very dramatic look, particularly when using tall-stemmed glass containers, as pictured here. These are perfect for filling huge ballrooms with flowers with dramatic effect while allowing seated guests at each table to see each other and talk across the table. Here, the large-headed 'Clooney' ranunculus are mixed with the gorgeous black 'Queen of the Night' tulips, and 'Extase' and 'Grand Prix' roses with a few deep red peonies. Trails of ivy has been placed across the tall, red martini-style glass vase to give rhythm to the arrangement and to make it look more natural.

RIGHT The development of the widespread production of these tall, thin glass vases, ranging from 24 to 48 inches, has been immensely influential on the decoration of ballrooms across the world. Simple but effective, this look is created by arranging layers of scrunched-up cellophane and petals, to which water is then added. The vase is topped with a tightly packed hand-tied arrangement of orange 'Wow,' green 'Jade,' lilac 'Coolwater,' red 'Passion,' and burgundy 'Black Baccara' roses.

Some of these ideas have been revisited over the years and have become very much a part of my own signature style. The flowers may change as new varieties appear, the style of vase may alter, and the colorways are amended quite dramatically, but the essential design remains.

PREVIOUS PAGES Vanda orchid and lilac skeletonized leaf has been wired onto a pearlized and elasticized bracelet. I discovered these bracelets in the United States, where florists are often asked to make wrist corsages for the senior prom.

A large, round summer hand-tied bouquet has been placed in one of our signature-style box carriers. This "just picked from the English garden border" look is one of my favorites. It includes peonies, dahlias, and 'Blue Pacific' and 'Sterling Silver' roses with stocks, agapanthus, and mixed with mint, *Viburnum tinus* berries, and *Alchemilla mollis*. It has been wrapped in Deconet and then aqua packed for safe transportation.

For a long time I had admired the very decorative gateaux designs that were a signature style of the Copenhagen florist Tage Anderson. Then, during a visit to a large floral relay corporation in the United States, I discovered that a rather mundane cake flower design had become the rage and was one of their best-selling items. When I returned home, I created my own version of the birthday cake, which now has become a perennial favorite of our design selection. The base is made from rosemary, although heather works equally well, and normally I use roses because they have a uniform head size; however, it can work just as well with small, round-headed summer flowers such as cornflowers, margarita daisies, and asters. Among the pink roses used here are 'Illusion,' 'Beauty By Oger,' 'Esperance,' 'Sweet Akito,' and the green rose, 'Jade.'

The topiary candelabra looks particularly good against a blank canvas and is perfect for wedding venues. Using flowers in season always creates the best and most emotional response from the observer, and once you have the metal frame you can add whatever seasonal decoration you like. In spring I add blossom, in summer, ivy and in winter, dried or painted twigs or heavily berried branches. The base of the candelabra has been covered with wet floral foam and moss. A round 12-inch wreath frame has been placed on the branches of the candelabra so that flowers can be added to the top. Wired around the metal frame are birch twigs with sprouting catkins and moss, to which lots of spring jasmine and ivy have been added. The frame has been highlighted with lots of lilac blossom and purple lisianthus and groups of 'Blue Pacific' roses. The stunning effect of cascading informality befits the romantic ambience that candlelight imbues.

These designs are massed with lots of flowers and foliage, giving a colorful textural impact. They are inspired by a love of the English cottage garden look.

ABOVE Using a simple design and repeating the idea is very effective, and it makes more visual impact. This trend has been a very popular theme in recent years, either using the same mixed selections of one flower or using just one type of flower. Rather than the flowers being grouped in arrangement, it is the containers that are displayed together. Here, mixed sweet peas have been hand tied and displayed in matching frosted glass vases.

RIGHT A perennially favorite color combination is pink, lilac, and lime green. This spiraled, hand-tied bouquet of pink astilbe, cerise 'Milano' roses, dahlias, peonies, hydrangea, and double purple lisianthus is made more vibrant by using the lime green foliages of fountain grass and *Viburnum opulus*. The spiky 'Green Revert' chrysanthemum has a slightly less acidic tone than the shamrock chrysanthemum that is often used.

This cube glass vase is so versatile and allows you to create many different feels within it. Here equisetum stems have been used in a uniform way to hide the green floral foam, and this combination of red 'Grand Prix' roses and green cymbidium orchids with burgundy roses is one of our most popular designs for Valentine's Day. For most of my designs, a third of the plant material is foliage, and as a general rule, I try to select three different types to add texture. Here, ivy berries blend with red skimmia and hebe.

I often go the fruit and vegetable market for inspiration, particularly in winter when the flower choice is more limited. I am particularly fond of the glaucous color and feel of the Savoy cabbage. I have been using Savoy cabbages as a basis for an arrangement for well over a decade. I core out the center and insert a styrofoam cup filled with floral foam. They look best filled with roses, and here 'Milano,' 'Wow,'and 'Grand Prix' have been arranged in the foam with a touch of red skimmia. Savoy cabbages look great sprayed gold or silver and filled with red or white roses respectively for the holiday season.

RIGHT Flower trends closely follow fashion, and when striped fabric was all the rage, soon enough we were creating very geometric flower arrangements. Plexiglas has been very popular as a container as it can be easily made in any size or color desired. Originally, the idea for this design came from designing a party with a black and white theme where I used white 'Akito' and 'Black Baccara' roses in low, oriental-style black dishes. The floral foam can be concealed with a raft of either straight twigs or reeds such as natural equisetum. The foam is also concealed by bright pink gravel, and rather than a checkerboard effect, this arrangement was created using diagonal lines of pink roses—working from the left, these are 'Dolce Vita,' 'Aqua,' 'Milano,' 'Pink Renate,' 'Poison,' and 'Milano.'

OPPOSITE This twiggy basket with glycerined oak leaves has been wired onto a sturdy basket. I use a supplier in Spain who makes some exquisite baskets, and I found ones that also combine ½–inch chicken wire, useful for building into structures like this or using to attach fruit. To this basket I have added some sumata wood, which is new to the floral market and is very much in demand. This sumata wood, which is usually more popular for continental or oriental designs, has been flocked to give it a furry colored coat. Here I have used brown, but I have seen it in the most vibrant shades of blue, lime green, red, and pink, as well as black. Into the basket I have snugly fitted a glass vase filled with water, packed around with moss. The roses, which include 'Beauty By Oger,' 'Halloween,' and 'Aroma' are mixed with miniature pink anthuriums. The dark red skimmia and a few brown rudbeckia heads bring the brown of the base through the arrangement.

LEFT This lavender basket has been in popular demand for June weddings for over ten years. There is something completely divine in being able to fashion the base out of this wonderful, scented flower. The small bunches of lavender have been tied with raffia to the basket, and the interior has been packed with moss. A plastic bowl filled with floral foam has been added to the top and filled with scented mint, blackberries, *Alchemilla mollis,* and masses of garden roses. This organic style works surprisingly well in modern interiors as well as rustic settings.

Classical topiary shapes always look good, and over the year it has become a trademark to use flowers and fruits or vegetables. This has the added advantage of giving great texture to the design, and it also can be better commercially since very often fruits and vegetables can be considerably less expensive than flowers to purchase. Here I have chosen eggplants because of their color and shiny texture. They are also quite firm and so are perfect for wiring into a moss frame. When choosing the flowers for a dense arrangement like this, it is advisable to use some larger–headed flowers or foliage to help cover the expanse. Here, ornamental cabbages make the perfect filler. Camellia leaves and skimmia also form the base with 'Aqua' and 'Avalanche' roses predominating the design. Pussy willow has been added along the contours of the design to give a more natural feel.

This arrangement started out as a design for a wedding where the bridegroom unusually was organizing the flowers as his bride was overseas. My brief from the client was for a large, round arrangement that included candles and that was low enough so that you could see across the table. When he also asked me to combine his favorite flowers, the tall birds of paradise, I had to go back to the workroom and try out a few sample ideas before coming up with this design. The birds of paradise were placed in a pinholder in the center of a straight-sided 12-inch glass dish. Water and floating candles were added. Around the edge of the dish I anchored a 14-inch floral foam ring, which was edged in galax leaves, and the base was greened with coral fern and *Viburnum tinus* berries. The South African foliages *Leucadendron* 'Safari Sunset' and 'Silver Brunia' were added for texture and visual interest. Groups of the brightly colored pink 'Milano,' orange 'Wow,' and pink orange 'Milva' roses were placed around the ring. The orange of the strelitzia was picked out with the textural leucospermum, and the purple was emphasized by groups of double purple lisianthus. Bright pink 'Serena' gerberas and short gloriosa flower heads completed the vibrant ring. The eye is brought from the base to the heads of the birds by using a few branches of contorted willow.

ABOVE Natural clay pots are always a winning container for flowers, and I am always drawn to old containers such as these oil pots from Provence. I have quite a collection of them, and this is one of my largest, which I have filled with foxgloves, coral and red peonies mixed with dark purple *Prunus*, and the dangly explosions of fountain grass. The grass softens the arrangement, and the flowers and foliage are in harmony with the vase. Frequently I find that this kind of classic arrangement will both suit traditional spaces and soften more contemporary interiors.

RIGHT For a long time I have been buying inexpensive lampshades as covers for vases for big events. I was first attracted to the lampshade when I found some being made from horizontal rings of ribbon by a local designer. These made such a perfect companion to the mixed flower posies that after that I often sought the lampshade department for inspiration. Here black satin shades have been filled with the large-headed burgundy 'Clooney' ranunculus and red peonies. The drama of the arrangement has been completed by using a ring of black feather boa. When the whole thing is encircled by small, red votive candleholders, it makes a very dramatic and romantic centerpiece.

These simple arrangements are often the ones that stand the test of time. New floral 'fads' come and go, but simple blocks of color always look good. These bow vases filled with one type and color of flower still look good fifteen years after the idea was first introduced.

These bow vases have remained one of my favorite vases for nearly two decades. They are very beautifully colored, handmade glass vases by the artist Paul Williams. I used a set linked together for my second book, and the photograph went on to become a very long-standing poster by a famous, worldwide Swedish furniture maker. These muted spring colors have been diagonally spaced, starting with yellow ranunculus, deep blue hydrangea, lime green 'Shamrock' chrysanthemums, deep blue hyacinths, and pale yellow 'Winterburg' tulips.

LEFT Sometimes clients leave the design and plant choices to me, giving me artistic license! Very often these have been times when new designs have emerged. This fishbowl arrangement was created for a charity competition among designers at the London flower market. I won first prize, and it has been one of my most imitated designs. 'Mango' calla lilies have been arranged with orange leucospermums in a bed of green berries from Thailand.

OPPOSITE This design was originally a collaboration with two of my designers, Anita Everard and Rachel Mashiter. Rare white spathiphyllum flowers from Holland have been teamed with pussy willow to make a round cage. Set in a low, frosted dish with floral foam concealed by white sand, the pussy willow has been shaped into a ball. The spathiphyllums have been placed in the foam and are bound onto the frame with silver aluminum wire. Adding a few blocks of glass ice completes this icy white look. I particularly like this design with green 'Midori' or 'Pistache' anthuriums.

BELOW I love boat-shaped containers for long dining room tables, and this is one of two I have by one of my favorite accessory companies, the Dutch firm DKHOME. The starkness of the black and silver lacquered vase is complemented by spray painting some contorted hazel silver and placing it through the fresh flower design. This delicate arrangement uses phalaenopsis orchids, eucharist lilies, white peonies, and double-headed peach hollyhocks to add a touch of pretty color.

part one

fundamentals

British *Vogue* once described me as "anarchic," and when describing my work, journalists will often say that I break all the rules. Before you can find your own floral style, you need to be grounded in many of the fundamentals, as they are the structure, the mechanics, and the method you need to know in order to be creative. As floristry is a living art form—which is most often also commercial—flower arrangers and florists need to understand and execute the basics to be able to move on artistically.

design rules

In short, you cannot really begin to break the rules until you know what the rules are. Although a lot of my arrangements are very simple in essence and some do break "perceived wisdom" on flower designing, I would always recommend any wannabe florist to learn all the basics and to study design work of many different florists from all over the world to gain a very broad view of the profession. Personally, I would like to see the standard of the profession ever rising, so whether you are charging for your services or not, it is your duty to present your designs in an imaginative yet competent and secure way, which is why you need to know and understand the fundamentals.

Good floral design in my opinion should be immediately attractive and appear effortless and natural—in other words, take a group of flowers and foliage that are individually appealing and create a composition that enhances their beauty. I can appreciate the work of many floral designers whose style and methods are quite different from my own, but it is my own personal conviction that the flowers should be the stars of the design and that the design should never be allowed to overpower the natural beauty of the flowers.

It is quite difficult to analyze the elements of good design in any art form, but basic design principles can be applied to all forms of art. In floral art a good design not only combines these design elements in its construction, but it also takes into consideration such factors as the occasion and the setting for which the flowers are intended, the purpose of the design, and the budget of the patron. Indeed, the *raison d'être* of any flower arrangement is the starting point for any floral designer. Flowers are always sent, given, or displayed to convey personal messages or to create an ambience. The floral designer has to have empathy with the client to be able to use the flowers appropriately to set the desired scene, or to convey the right emotion. Effective floral design has to marry all these elements, making sure that the material, the design, and the location are all harmonious and on budget!

The floral foam ring is immensely useful for decorative floristry. Here a 14-inch frame has been used to create an arrangement with two levels of interest. The base is full of textural flowers such as blue-green hydrangea, dracaena leaves, flowering eucalptus, and eryngium. Groups of three 'Grand Prix' and 'Coolwater' roses are placed at different heights and levels around the ring. Four purple pillar candles are wired into the frame and nine tall purple 'French' tulips are placed around the ring in three groups placed in a natural vegetative way.

Making the vase part of the arrangement has been a trademark of mine since I began floristry, and every year there are new styles of vases to arouse our creativity. The widespread arrival of a very light aluminum wire available in many bright colors as well as metallic bronze, silver, and gold inspired this new design, in which orchids can be suspended throughout the vase. A hand-tied arrangement of pink phalaenopsis orchids, edged with anthurium leaves and bound bymore aluminum wire, tops the vase.

shape and form

There are three factors that underlie all good floral composition: form, color, and function. There is an enormous diversity of shapes, form, and patterns in the plant world, and some study of flowers, plants, and trees in their natural habitat will be invaluable for creating good floral design. Before I became addicted to floral design, I was in love with nature and spent most my early childhood enjoying the outdoor life in my home county of Suffolk, England. The organic world has been a powerful source of inspiration to artists of all disciplines throughout history, and in my opinion, many forms in nature are the best shapes to emulate. The shape of a tree, the structure of plants, individual flower heads, grasses, leaf and flower patterns—they are all inspirational for new designs.

In my floral work I like using styles that take a very holistic approach and display the flowers as if they were growing. This works particularly well for arrangements on windows or mantelpieces or even small landscapes on tables. These designs are very suitable for informal arrangements with a wildflower feel. I have also found much inspiration in the vegetable patch or trips to fruit and vegetable markets and frequently incorporate cabbages and cauliflowers in my work. Most floral designs will feature a number of different attractive forms displayed together.

Hundreds of different shapes and forms of flower arrangements, but not all, have clear-cut definitions or easy descriptions. However, there are some everyday designs that will be the first shapes and forms you will learn to make. First, you need to decide whether the arrangement you wish to create will be round or front facing. Round arrangements can be viewed from all sides, while front-facing ones will normally be displayed against a wall or on a mantel so that all of the interest is concentrated on one side.

The next decision will be whether you wish to create a formal or informal arrangement. Do you want something with strict geometric lines or something loose and freeflowing? Sometimes it may be easier to create a loose natural display than a more formal one. However, creating a successful informal arrangement can be much harder than making a very geometric formal arrangement.

mass style

This is the first of the two main arrangement forms in floral design, where there is little space in the arrangement, such as a dome of roses or a tightly arranged topiary. The mass style has its origins in Europe and is often considered very English. Inspiration for this type of work may have been drawn from early still life paintings, particularly the work of the seventeenth-century Flemish and Dutch painters. The Victorians especially loved the formal style of mass arrangements, and they designed and created many silver vases to hold their displays. It is currently more fashionable to use this style of arrangement in a much more loose and informal way.

Within the massed style, there are many different forms. It could be a simple bunch of mixed flowers in a vase or a dome of one type of flower, such as a tulip or ranunculus. These massed displays are generally known as "posy" or "domed." Traditionally, these were also referred to as "Biedermeier" designs and originally consisted of concentric circles of flowers with a collar of foliage.

The traditional massed arrangement can be made using either foam or chicken wire and can encompass small and large designs; from an arrangement for a small alcove to a trailing mantelpiece or pedestal arrangement. In most cases, this style has an upright axis that relies on line material. Dominant focal flowers are added, before finishing with "filler" material for an overall massed effect.

This massed topiary is a popular form and has been created by cementing a birch pole into a plastic pot and then spray painting it silver. The plastic pot is placed in a glass cylinder and then concealed by layers of brightly colored aggregate. A floral foam ball has been taped and wired securely on the top. A base of flowering eucalyptus, skimmia, and ivy berries have been added all around the foam ball, and a selection of gerberas in shades of pink massed over the top.

LEFT The Victorian posy—where massed flowers are placed in concentric circles—is a classic design and one that traditionally was often wired together. This one has been hand tied by working circles around a central rose. Widow iris, blue muscari, and white narcissus follow. The posy is then edged with massed violets.

It is also possible to make hand-tied bouquets in the line style, and I tend to sell more of this design as "masculine" hand-tied arrangements, intended for male recipients. I believe the line style shows off architectural flowers such as strelitzias, agapanthus, and other tropical flowers to their best advantage. I can understand why it is more popular in countries where more colorful flowers such as these grow, and also where there are fewer herbaceous flowers.

Within the line form there are many different styles. The most common is the architectural vertical arrangement. As I have already noted, the Japanese style of ikebana also falls under this style.

line-mass
This style of arrangement uses flowers in larger massed groups, and it was in the 1950s and 1960s that this style of work became very popular. Constance Spry and Julia Clements pioneered flower arrangements and popularized arranging flowers in the home as an artistically satisfying experience. It was also in the 1950s that floral foam was invented, allowing amateur flower arrangers the opportunity to create a more structured arrangement; hence, popularity for line-mass arrangements was, in some ways, dictated by the new mechanics that became available at the time. Currently, the line-mass style is much more popular than the straightforward line arrangement.

Within the spectrum of the line-mass style there are many forms of flower arrangements that one can create, and in some ways the early teachers prescribed a code that has been slavishly reproduced to this day. Although one has to learn some rules, this so-called code for flower arranging has been regarded by some as too stifling and rigid, and many feel it is responsible for producing flower arrangements that are not very visually pleasing. There are

Massed flower heads may also be used in topiaries. This ancient art form originated in Eastern Europe, and the cone-shaped topiaries are often known as Byzantine. The shape is either fashioned by moss or foam, and the flowers, leaves, and sometimes fruits are pinned or placed in the moss or foam. The use of moss allows the designer to mold any shape. This technique is suitable for very large arrangements for special events where the life of the arrangement is usually quite short.

line form
The line form style is usually a formal arrangement using tall flowers and structural plant material. There is far more open space, and only part of the shape is filled with flowers and foliages. This style of arrangement originated from the East, most notably China and Japan. It is not known precisely when the line style was adopted in the West, but the first Japanese ikebana arrangements are recorded as being shown at London's Chelsea Flower Show in 1912, and it was sometime in the 1950s that Americans started to take an interest in the Eastern style, with line arrangement reaching a peak in the mid-1970s.

many designs that fall into this category, and it is necessary for any student of floristry to be aware of them.

the symmetrical triangle
One of the most popular line-mass arrangements, which, in my opinion, is one of the least attractive.

the asymmetrical triangle
This can be a useful arrangement to create at either end of a mantelpiece, but I would almost always veer toward a massed asymmetrical arrangement.

the crescent shape
This is a moon-shaped design that is normally constructed in a shallow dish. A clever choice of plant material is required for this design to be successful, and it is a testing choice of arrangement for any student to make well.

the Hogarth curve
So called because the artist William Hogarth described an elongated "S" as a line of beauty. This is an interesting shape in and of itself, and with the right plant material it can be visually pleasing.

parallel style
This is a style that has been very influenced by European floristry, in which the mechanics generally include a rectangular block of foam set in a shallow dish, from which groups arise vertically. I like this style when the designer tries to make the arrangement as natural as possible, but am less in favor of very structured versions. This is an interesting technique that is generally more important in competitive floristry than in the wider commercial world.

the deconstructed style
A recent fashion in floral design, this involves taking a number of vases collected together either to display one flower head or a group of flowers. In its most extreme form, this style can be a way of

using petals to construct a flower or a design; for example, using flower heads to create a lei or a daisy chain. It takes some inspiration from Asian cultures and their traditions in flower arranging.

Many of my designs would be classed as unconventional or free style—they do not fit any particular category, and they are not bound by any rules of design. They are often inspired by fashion, art, architecture, and design and are very popular currently. Contained arrangements are also in vogue, where all rules about the size of the container in relation to the arrangement are abandoned, and the flowers are used inside a glass vase.

BELOW The current trend in floral design is for deconstructed arrangements. This is an example of where the arrangement is actually in the vase and almost the antithesis of perceived floristry rules. The Victorians were crazy about terrariums, indoor glass gardens, and artificial flowers in huge glass domes. In the 1970s, bottle gardens were all the rage, and now the manufacture of huge glass vases has created the vogue for arrangements of cut flowers within the vase. Here eight yellow calla lilies have been arrangemd with three small monstera leaves.

balance

Balance in flower arranging is about physical balance and visual balance. Physical balance is obviously very important when creating an arrangement to keep the whole thing stable, particularly when creating a large pedestal or mantelpiece arrangement for a special event. Poorly constructed arrangements can topple over and be a danger. Whether you are using foam or a vase or even creating a hand-tied bouquet, you need to make sure that the plant material is placed to spread the weight over the entire area of design.

Studying nature can help enormously in understanding visual balance. Regard the density of a group of reeds growing together, take inspiration from the scale of a stem of a flag iris in relation to its bloom, enjoy the patterns of magnolia blossom in early spring. By using nature as your guide, you will be able to create beautifully balanced arrangements.

Visual balance is more complicated to explain. In general, the eye is drawn to the area in a design that is perceived to contain the most interest. The materials in a visually balanced design will be arranged around an imaginary vertical or horizontal axis so the eye is drawn equally to both sides. Using equal amounts of flowers may create symmetry or make a design look rigid; as a guide, choose darker flowers, which look heavier than pale ones, or use round flowers that look heavier than trumpet shapes. In a large design, tall delphiniums and digitalis can be visually balanced by trailing amaranthus or ivy over the edge of the base of the design. The movement created by the foliage counterbalances the strong linear flowers, adding texture and softness. The incorrect placement of plant material will make a design look unbalanced or at worst, unattractive or even ugly.

This tall, thin vase arrangement has actual balance so that the weight of the fritillarias are equally weighted to make the vase stable. The willow gives more visual balance to the overall look, and the collar of lilac hydrangea gives stability in real terms and also visually.

harmony

Harmony is a hard concept to describe and a quality that is in some ways intensely personal. A harmonious arrangement is one that is artistically pleasing and where all the natural elements of the design work together well. It is the quality I look for when accessing the work of a floral designer of a very different style from my own. A harmonious result is achieved when balance, scale, repetition, rhythm, and proportion all effectively work together. In other words, none of the design rules should conflict. The most useful way to understand harmony is to look at combinations of materials

When selecting flowers and foliages for a vase, focus on the color and proportion of the flowers to give a pleasing shape with a good outline and a natural feel. This harmonious vase combines seasonal flowers in greens, pinks, and lilac, and includes a good mix of shapes such as the tall delphiniums, the round 'Shamrock' chrysanthemums, and peony tulips, with lilac and guelder rose to fill. Light tendrils and buds of lisianthus lighten the outline while the solomon's seal creates a soft edge between arrangement and vase.

as they are found in nature. For example, if you created a spring woodland scene using a combination of moss, bark, cowslips, violets, and primroses, the harmonious balance would be lost by adding a commercially grown rose.

A fresh bunch of cow parsley in an pottery pitcher displayed in a rural cottage is in harmony to its surroundings. Often the simplest and most uncontrived arrangements are the most successful in achieving overall harmony. Too much variety of plant material, overuse of accessories, and overworked designs are apt to confuse and often destroy the effect of harmony.

The brown, green, and sandy shades of these beans have been matched by the hand- tied posy at the top, which includes peonies, dahlias, fountain grass, hydrangea, *Alchemilla mollis*, and green dill. The base looks rustic and is in harmony with the flower choice.

There are many occasions where the simplicity of using all-white cut flowers looks absolutely stunning. I particularly like to use white with a minimum of green so the effect is more arresting. I also love to use white flowers in frosted vases to give a very clean feel to the design. Here twenty-five heads of white phalaenopsis orchid have been hand tied with three small monsteria leaves and then placed in an elegant frosted vase. The proportion of the spray of these delicate flowers perfectly complements the elegantly tall vase.

scale and proportion

For an arrangement to be in proportion, there needs to be the right mix of elements, whereby the plant materials need to relate well, and both the dimensions and quantities of the design should be in proper scale with the chosen surroundings. Proportion is also a vital consideration for choosing both the container and the flower. For centuries—in fact ever since the foundations for good proportion were laid down by the ancient Greeks—a formula has been established, which has been considered as a pleasing proportion. The golden "section" or "ration" suggests that proportion should be about 1:6, and over time this led to flower design rules being laid down that suggest that the flowers would be 1½ times the height of the container. Although this benchmark may still be considered for competitive flower arranging, I think that this formula, which was originally applied to the proportions of the human body and which fundamentally was applied to architecture, cannot be rigidly applied to an organic art form such as floral design. It is more theoretically interesting than practical. Certainly, it allows designers to create classical design of great proportion, but it is

BELOW This very classical arrangement of greenery and creams includes gardenia foliage, guelder roses, lilac, and 'Avalanche' and 'Alexis' roses. These grouped flowers are in perfect proportion to the silver bowl as they are about 1½ times higher than the container. You develop a sense of proportion and balance as you progress with your flower-arranging skills—getting the proportion wrong a few times is usually the fastest way to learn good proportion!

equally to the interior space for which it is intended. A large, white space will suit a bold arrangement. Similarly, a dark paneled room will require an equally bold statement in order to compete with the interior.

While adopting these general principles for proportion, some designers like the challenge of creating large designs from flowers and plants of tiny proportions. Small plants or flowers heads are then massed and placed in tall structures. The most commonly used and popular arrangements of this type is one in which the mass of proportions is upright. Examples of upward proportions include large, classical pedestal arrangements; most vase arrangements; line arrangements; and parallel, natural, and vegetative arrangements.

In my own work, I am fond of the upright proportions, but since I like my arrangements to be quite natural, my upright arrangements are asymmetrical and weighted in proportion by trailing foliages and flowers. I love very droopy arrangements where the emphasis of the proportion is downward, and where the greenery and flowers cascade in a waterfall effect. Several arrangements command this look, and among them are the trailing arrangement above a fireplace and the droopy, low arrangement that is traditionally positioned at the front of the bride and groom's table at a wedding. For a less happy occasion, I use flower designs with downward proportions when creating a spray to place on top of a coffin, which can also trail over the sides.

Horizontal proportion is often used for low table arrangements, side tables, or for corporate work. This is far more popular in designer floristry than in the everyday bread-and-butter work of a florist. When a designer creates a ball or spherical shape, he or she is creating an arrangement of symmetrical proportion. The density of the plant material is uniform, so visually it has the same proportion through the entirety of the shape.

ABOVE It is very important that the flowers chosen are in perfect scale to the vase, so for this miniature urn I have chosen to use the dimunitive snake's head fritillarias. I am often asked which comes first—the container or the flowers—and generally I prefer to take my inspiration from the flowers and then decide on the container.

too rigid for the inspirational floral designer. It also takes no account of the constant change in fashion and also the different ways that most of today's top floral designers create their own organic containers.

Whichever way you approach the design, the flowers, the foliage, and the container all have to be in proportion to the design. Usually the space determines the overall size of the arrangement, and then a suitable container is chosen. With this established, the designer then chooses plant materials that are in proportion to the container and the desired size of the arrangement. This is important both in terms of the size and scale of the flowers as well as their color. Some colors may dominate the flower choice and also change the visual proportion of the arrangement; this applies

For larger classical arrangements, it is important to use tall and large-headed flowers to keep the arrangement in proportion to the vase or, in this case, urn. Large star-haped cream 'Concordia' lilies with tall branches of forsythia and foxglove give height. Huge heads of hydrangea, coral peonies, and chrysanthmums make a good impact and look appropriate in the sturdy verdigris urn. The fountain grass and cream hypericum provide a soft edge around the urn and add downward proportion.

texture and contrast

Putting a group of flowers together with the same textures and creating a bunch or a tightly packed area gives enormous impact to any kind of design and is favored in contemporary floristry. The grouping of plant material of the same color and type in tight groups is also sometimes referred to as blocking. Next to color, texture is one of the most important decisions when putting together a group of flowers for any design. I love to create patchworks or blocks of texture, and when planning a list for purchasing flowers at the market, I always try to include as many textures as I can to give the composition depth. I usually achieve this even in very inexpensive arrangements by using at least three different types of foliage, with five being my preferred

number. Plant material comes in lots of different textures: some flowers and leaves are glossy, such as bright red 'Tropical' anthuriums and waxy green monstera leaves. Some almost have the texture of fabric: the heads of celosia look like woven chenille and are available in many gorgeous colors; the texture and pattern on the leaves of the *Anthurium crystallinum* is quite astounding and can be so dominant in a design that it dictates a strong choice of accompanying flowers to complement its own strong form and texture.

One textural favorite of mine is the pincushion protea *Leucopsernum cordifolio*, which pops up again and again in my work and designs. I love the contrast of its spiky and furry flowers against the deep, velvety texture of

BELOW This ring is full of textures, from the soft and furry leucospermums to the velvety 'Circus' and 'Cherry Brandy' roses. The lotus seed heads have lovely markings almost like showerheads, while some of the foliage is shiny, such as the galax leaves and the folded aspidistra. The berries of the 'Red Flair' hypericum are bright and glossy, and the guelder rose and white skimmia with their small flowerets give the ring some lightness and movement. The elegant 'Mango' callas and the Flexi grass give the dense foliage contrast and add richness and impact to the overall design.

roses, or next to the dense flower heads of the gerbera daisy. Prickly flowers such as the artichoke flower *Cynara scolymus* need strong flowers to complement their striking and strong character. Fluffy or feathery flowers such as gypsophilia or the South African *Serruria florida* need to be mixed with strong, regular shapes, such as roses or carnations.

Contrast refers to the different effect created when two pieces of plant material are placed next to one another. Sometimes a design requires a diversity of plant material. A large, round classic pedestal for a celebration requires contrasting forms of flowers; for example, round shapes, star shapes, and

spires, mixed with contrasting foliage. A contrast of texture is achieved when one piece of plant material is of a different density to the one placed next to it. A shiny surface is more compelling to the eye than a rough texture. This is particularly useful when creating designs with a monochromatic theme. The different colors, shades, and tints of plant material can also be used to create a striking contrast. Being placed next to a matte leaf or branch will enhance any bright flower. I love to create contrast in my designs and therefore deliberately choose to use contrasting colors and textures; very often the result is a rich and dramatic arrangement.

ABOVE The delicate white flowers of eucharis and jasmine in this simple hand-tied bouquet contrasts with some hebe, *Garrya elliptica*, and one of my favorite textural foliages, *Senecio greyii*. By contrasting the delicate against the dense, you often create a surprisingly arresting result.

movement

A good-looking design uses techniques and materials that move the eye from one part of the display to the next. When there is rhythm in the design, there is movement to the eye, allowing the arrangement to appear natural and alive. Without movement, an arrangement can look static, artificial, and unattractive. There are some accepted ways of getting movement into an arrangement, one of which is to use some curved and natural-looking stems and plant material. Choose various sized blooms so the flower head size is not too regular. As a rule, use at least three different types of foliage, preferably five, and make sure they are of contrasting sizes and shapes and include at least one with texture such as blossom or

berries. It is a good idea to choose flowers at various stages in their development. Spray flowers such as roses or lisianthus enhance a sense of movement. When you place the plant material, make sure you use some to recede into the arrangement as well as placing some on the outer extremities of the design. Try to hide all straight stems, which may make the arrangement look rigid.

The effect of movement is created through the use of line and color in the design and by executing repetition or graduation. This principle gives flow to the arrangement and encourages the eye to move along and through the container. Here, the trailing shape of the pink phalaenopsis orchids and dyed vine give movement to a contemporary arrangement in a simple vase.

dominance

In most arrangements, with the exception of round arrangements, there is an area of dominance that is known as the focal point, center of growth, or center of interest. It is the area of the arrangement to which the eye is drawn. Traditionally, there was only one area of dominance because too many competing dominant areas of one arrangement can be confusing to the eye. Usually the focal point is a choice flower or group of flowers or the area from which all the stems appear to radiate. In contemporary floristry, a number of attractive alternatives have evolved, providing many diverse areas where the eye may be drawn and where there may be several points of interest. These focal points may be below the container in a trailing arrangement, in the container of a horizontal arrangement, or way above the container of a standing bouquet.

Cymbidium orchids would normally be most dominant in an arrangement because they are large, have many heads, and are visually very arresting. The use of the folded pandanus leaves subordinates the orchids, changing the visual dominance within the overall arrangement.

The phormium leaves weaving throughout this long, low horizontal design take the eye through the composition and out to the peach tulips.

rhythm

Rhythm in music gives a composition its feeling and flow and also stimulates the visual senses and imagination. It is exactly the same for a flower arrangement. Rhythm gives movement to a design, making it more pleasing to the eye. The perceived rhythm can come from the progression of one flower or one type of foliage throughout the arrangement. This flower or foliage creates a strong visual line. Rhythm gives excitement to an arrangement, which may otherwise look solid or fragmented. Three other elements can add rhythm:

1   Repetition of a group of flowers or of a design. Repetition is one of my favorite devices for this and can be achieved by using groupings of materials in an arrangement or groupings of the same arrangement. Usually the same type of flower or color is grouped together to create the repetition of an idea. This immediately enhances the single design.

2   Transitional flowers and foliages are important to the study of rhythm because they complement the lines of the design and allow the eye to travel easily from one part of the design to the other. Flower size and color play an important part in achieving good transition. A great arrangement allows the transition from one piece of plant material to the next to occur as unobtrusively as possible.

3   The plant material should all radiate from a central point of the growth. This gives the arrangement elegance and grace and makes the rhythm of the design look natural.

ABOVE I love this boat-shaped container: the arched pussy willow has been prized into the two ends of the boat to fit snugly, and cymbidium orchid heads have been arranged along the length. The eye is drawn naturally across the willow from one flower head to another.

Color blocking has always been an important visual look for the commercial florist and can look very effective in a hotel foyer as well as for a celebration. Three red, glass tear vases have been topped with round floral foam balls decorated with small gerbera daisies know as 'Germini.' These chunky arrangements are made visually more attractive by the design being repeated. Odd numbers of designs work better than even ones, particularly with symmetrical designs like these.

repetition

The repeating of elements in floral design, currently very popular in contemporary floristry, creates a feeling of movement and adds color and textural interest to the design, giving it stronger visual impact. Today there is a vogue to repeat a simple design by placing one, two, three, or even more identical arrangements together. This incredibly simple idea may comprise something as simple as the placement of stems in a group—it is the repetition that gives the groups visual strength. Thirty bubble vases placed together with one marguerite daisy in each is more arresting that one vase with thirty stems. A group of narcissus arranged as living topiaries looks stunning down the center of a long table or across a mantel. Also currently very fashionable is to use the repetition of color by placing three or five or even more glass vases together and massing one variety in one color in each vase.

ABOVE Two very simple vase arrangements are grouped together for more visual impact. Each vase has a bunch of Iranian dogwood, one cymbidium orchid, and one monstera leaf. The visual lines are repeated and the plant material looks more impressive in two vases than it would in one. As these arrangements are very asymmetrical, they look fine arranged in odd numbers.

Bunches of violets have
been edged with wired,
and skeletonized lilac leaves
and then bound together
to create this small
textural massed posy.

massing flowers

Floral designs, in which a mass of one material is used with very little space, have been popular at different times throughout floristry history, and flowers have always been massed by florists to create funeral tribute work, when the massing of heads together allows the florist to create shapes and letters. However, the widespread massing of flowers for all types of arrangements and celebrations is now very popular with flower arrangers all over the world. The impact is very immediate as there is a mass of color and texture. The individual line or form is not seen, only the mass of flowers. Massed flowers can take the form of an arrangement in foam, such as the posy pad pictured below left, or on an oasis ball like the gerberas below right. Alternatively, they can be hand tied, as in the vase arrangement pictured opposite or wired as in the rose and ivy posy pictured right. Whatever the methodology, the visual impact is very strong, and at some point, all types of florists, however different their styles, will use massed flowers.

ABOVE Twenty 'Iceberg' roses have been hand tied into a domed posy and then edged with trails of variegated ivy to soften the edge of the vase.

FAR LEFT A posy pad has been edged with galax leaves, and then massed chrysanthemum heads have been placed in the soaked floral foam. The floral tribute has been topped with a spray of 'Black Baccara' roses with forget-me-nots, lilac, and sweet peas.

LEFT A round bowl has been filled with bright pink aluminum wire and topped with a large floral foam ball massed with pink 'Serena' gerberas to form a massed table centerpiece.

grouping

Grouping flowers is perhaps the single most important technique for creating contemporary arrangements. Rather than mix a group of flowers through an arrangement, they are placed in groups, which creates a stronger visual flower arrangement. In classical work, flowers are often grouped to create a greater visual mass or for prompting a focal point. Grouped flowers may also be used in topiary shapes, whether round or spherical.

The contemporary practice has been led by the desire to use diverse and unusual color collections. Grouping flowers lets you use colors that would be visually unpleasing in more traditional, scattered arrangements. In a grouped arrangement you can place greenery or a complementary color next to one group of flowers so that you create peace between colors that do not look good together. I like the device of using dark-colored flowers such as black and burgundy and placing them next to brightly colored flowers such as magenta, orange, and lime to achieve really colorful designs. The key is the nature of the balance; it is not necessary to always group in odd numbers but do make sure there is great visual balance. Working with groups suits my own style of design as I love pushing back the boundaries of traditional color sense and because, quite simply, I love bright colors.

BELOW I have chosen to contrast the pale peach 'Toscana' rose with the dark burgundy 'Black Baccara' rose. The almost black dracaena leaf that covers the bowl, and the black ivy berries help to enhance the groupings of the colors. White lilac, lime-green guelder roses, and cymbidium orchids are used in equal balance to create a rich texture. This unusual color combination is visually enhanced by the tight groupings.

This is a very classic urn table arrangement using glossy green camellia foliage with groups of 'Avalanche' and 'Alexis' roses, mixed with white lilac, lime-green guelda roses, and white 'Diamond' bouvardia.

bunching and bundling

Bunching involves taking a group of the same variety of flowers and placing them together to create one unit. The bunches can then be placed in an arrangement with ribbon or raffia, or wired into a design. This bunching is also a textural device and can create more interest in an arrangement where there is a limited choice of floral material. It is also very suitable for very short flowers such as snowdrops and violets, which can then be pinned into a design. Bunching has its traditions in the English country house style where lavender, wheat, and barley were often used, and is still commonly used for dried flower arrangements. Generally, plant material chosen for bunching is long lasting and can exist without water for a while, which is why twigs and cinnamon are popular, or long-lasting foliage such as bamboo or equisetum. In late summer, late-harvested lavender or wheat can be used, which will then dry out naturally.

Bundling is the term given to tying together a number of stems for ornamental effect. Sometimes bundling can make use of a waste product like the end of stems or smaller lengths of material that have been disregarded for a design. For example, I often bundle up cinnamon sticks to use in winter flower arrangements. Bunches of dogwood or equisetum also create an interesting effect in a winter design. The tie itself can also add color to the arrangement, so that if you wish to add a bright color, you can incorporate an appropriate tie in colored wire or fabric. If you want the bundling to look as natural as possible, raffia or grass may be used.

BELOW LEFT Bundling is the design technique in which quantities of material are firmly bound together to create a pattern above the binding point and sometimes below. A sheaf of wheat is an example of a bundle in which stems radiate above the binding point and also below. Here these lovely pink calla lilies have been bunched together to create two areas of interest above the binding point of bright pink aluminum wire. This simple bunched design would be a stylish, contemporary bridal bouquet worn with a simple wedding gown or may also work in an elegant vase.

RIGHT Binding or wiring several of the same plant materials together and wiring them into an arrangement is a technique traditionally used for garlands. Many wood carvings that date back to the Elizabethan period depict early forms of this bunching. This technique is more likely to be used in midsummer when there are lots of seed heads and herbs around or in midwinter when making garlands using either cinnamon sticks or groups of dried and sprayed bunches of twigs. Here fresh lavender has been bunched into a swag with wired fennel bulbs to create a lovely natural garden feel. Green and white hydrangea and blowsy garden roses are grouped on a base of *Viburnum tinus* berries.

carpeting

This technique is most often used to create low table centerpiece designs or as a base for more vertical placements, when it is sometimes known as the groundwork. Variations of textures are used to create very short stems of plant material. Patterns of lines are crafted using moss, twigs, textural foliages, and flower heads. Carpeting can afford some variations in height, but I prefer this style when it is low and tactile, like a collage. This floristry technique is used more in winter when plant material is less available or when a florist wants to set a theme.

pave This is a term borrowed from jewelry designers and refers to the use of setting stones close together so that no metal is visible. In floristry, paving refers to covering the surface of a design or an object such as a sphere with a mass of plant material so that it creates a uniform area with little variation of depth. The most common application of this technique is to cover spherical balls with bun moss or chrysanthemums such as the tiny uniform 'Santini' varieties. The effect of such plant material is to create a flat "cobblestone" surface. The materials chosen for this can be floral and freshly cut or dried. Leaves, fruit, pods, berries, vegetables, mosses, legumes, and even stones are used. Fresh flowers and foliage are usually arranged into green floral foam, whereas dried material may be pinned or wired or occasionally glued.

BELOW This very contemporary table centerpiece uses the heavy contrast of the diagonally cut cigar reeds *Cannomois virgata* against the very delicate cappuccino-specked pink ranunculus and balls of fluffy green *Viburnum opulus*.

layering

This technique is by no means a new one in floristry and was originally used as far back as ancient Egypt. Layering flowers, leaves, and fruit is still popular in many cultures. In Hawaii, it is customary to thread flowers to create leis.

In southern Europe, bay leaves are threaded onto string to dry out, and in South America, chilies are threaded in rows to dry. Today, the most commonly used layering technique uses overlapping leaves to hide the wire. Some floral artists use glue to stick the leaves, but I am rather adverse to the glue gun, only getting it out for the holiday season or when all other methods have failed. My preference is to use double-sided tape to layer leaves onto containers to create sculptural containers. Traditionally, layering was used to create military decorations, and it is now used most notably in sympathy work to make floral chaplets. It now has a wider audience due to themed parties and the demand for more sculptural pieces that are often designed for large event work.

ABOVE This garland of carnation heads and galaxy leaves has been strung onto a heavy florist wire. The wire goes into the top of the stem and through the ovary of the flower and out through the top of the corolla, onto which the next flower or leaf is strung, creating a layered effect.

LEFT This floral foam heart topped with roses has been edged with layered glossy camellia leaves. They have been placed slightly on top of each other so that they create a layered effect, giving depth and movement to the pinned leaves. Most often one leaf is laid on top of the next to conceal the pinning.

manipulating plant material

Winding arrangements became fashionable at the end of the twentieth century and have been adopted with a passion ever since. Starting with natural materials, the technique progressed to accessories until everything became wrapped up and constricted! You have to have a certain temperament to be good at this kind of work, because it is very time consuming. It is also more relevant to specialized floral design than everyday work because of the labor costs in creating these pieces.

leaf weaving & manipulation

There are many types of plant material that lend themselves to be woven or bent to enhance a display. I was first fascinated by this art of leaf weaving and manipulation on a trip to Thailand and have since incorporated it in simple ways in my own designs. Galax, ivy, aspidistra, aralia, flax, and grasses, in particular, steel, lily and flexi grass, are all suitable plant materials. Equisetum has very graphic lines and is one of the most commonly used. The Victorians nicknamed the aspidistra plant "the cast iron plant," and it is one of my favorites for bending around the end of hand-tied bouquets or for concealing containers. It is inexpensive, long lasting, and so durable. It can be bent, or the stem can be used to pierce the leaf to form a curve. Round leaves such as bergenia or galax can be formed into a cone shape or roll. Sculptural forms can be made by plaiting palms such as areca or kentia, but this form of manipulation is best left to the experts.

BELOW My favorite aspidistra leaf has been bent around a small collection of bright pink peonies, gloriosa, and *Viburnum opulus*. These leaves are inexpensive and create a lovely collar for a few flowers, making it seem a far more extravagant and gorgeous bouquet. The organza ribbon bow is one of my own, which I use especially for Valentine's Day. It has the lovely Goethe inscription: "The flower is a leaf made with love!"

This design was first created for the fortieth birthday party of a New Zealander who wanted to use native phormium in her party decorations. The New Zealand flax is extremely versatile and lasts very well so this has been used for numerous weddings and parties, but is also a favorite for our corporate work. Here, the pink 'Telstar' amaryllis have been supported internally by a bamboo garden stake, which helps the hollow stems hold the weight of the heavily hybridized head and also keeps the stems firmly anchored into the foam. Bun moss has been pinned onto the floral foam to hide the mechanics of the arrangement.

BELOW It is both in spring and autumn time—when the branches are either just starting to sprout or leafless—that I am drawn to making structures. Here, I have used Japanese magnolia branches about to burst with their blossom with orange tulips and *Euphorbia fulgens.*

This simple treelike structure is inspired by the leafless spring magnolias, which look so effective and grand. Aluminum wire has been wound around glass test tubes so they can be attached to contorted branches of hazel to hold water for the lisianthus. Cymbidium orchids and gerberas are also very effective in this design.

OPPOSITE This structure is made of white-leaved sorbus branches, just about to burst with their lovely soft green leaves. Long French peach tulips emphasize the structure, and soft-petaled peach roses line the base of floral foam at the top of the mossed basket.

structural designing

Flower structures are created by tying, twisting, threading, and wedging. Creating structure from plant material has become increasing popular over the last twenty-five years; this is a time-consuming and complex way to arrange flowers and has great popularity among competitive floristry. This includes bending and even clamping plant material. Raffia, string, or wire are used to secure these natural frames together. Shallow containers, organic-looking pots, or glass are ideal vehicles for structural designs. Often the container may be completely concealed by plant material.

Some structures are decorative, and some are used as mechanics. For example, a grid of dogwood over a vase can be used as mechanics for an arrangement. A cage can be constructed to contain flowers. Plant material with pliable stems is popular for these kinds of constructions, such as willow, trailing rose, eucalyptus, kerria, and vines such as honeysuckle, jasmine, clematis, and kiwi. Tough trailing greenery, such as passion flower, jasmine, ivy, smilax, ferns, and ruscus, and dried sticks and reeds, such as thin mikado sticks, are also very efffective for this type of work.

This style of floristry is too fussy and labor intensive for both my patience and my design aesthetic, but there are elements that I do use. Many of the principles can be applied to more everyday floristry and even to hand-tied bouquets. The ball of pussy willow and spathiphyllum on page 29 and the magnolia opposite are structures that have been designed to draw the eye into the center of the arrangement and to emphasize the beauty of the plant material used for the construction. Willow is very supple when the sap is rising in the spring and falling in the winter, so this plant material leads you to work during these seasonal times. Japanese magnolia flowers before the leaf appears, so it is particularly attractive to work with in the spring.

season

The wide selection of flowers available to today's consumer is largely unseasonal, with the top sellers distributing flowers such as roses, chrysanthemums, carnations, and alstromeria across the world. Being largely cultivated and heavily hybridized, they are available all year round with absolutely no discernible "best" season. However, for the flower arranger and the florist, there is still a wealth of seasonal produce; from the first clutch of English snowdrops, to the exquisite scent of narcissus from the Channel Isles or the first few bunches of mimosa from Italy.

It is also the seasonal change within foliage types that hugely influences floral design. In spring, the leafless branches sprout into action, and in fall, colorful foliages arouse new designs. The full-leaf foliages in midsummer encourage more classical full-blown style arrangements, and the limitations on flowers in the winter motivate designs based on evergreens. As the year unfolds there is a seasonally rich palette of color and texture.

For this spring arrangement, a collar of contorted willow has been fashioned by twisting together lengths into a wreath frame. Designed to sit on the edge of a frosted vase, it enhances the magnificent seasonal crown imperials.

OPPOSITE FAR LEFT This early summer arrangement is constructed by using a hand-tied posy of yellow and red achillea, strawberry-red godetia, variegated mint, lime-green *Alchemilla mollis, Viburnum opulus,* sprigs of rosemary, and garden roses. It has been placed on top of a glass bowl filled with fruits and water.

OPPOSITE LEFT This cube arrangement is one of my most versatile designs and can be made in any seasonal style. For this autumnal vase, we have lined a block of floral foam with red dogwood and then filled it with red skimmia and rosehips, groups of ruby red roses and 'Alexis' roses, and cymbidium orchids.

Traditionally, these forced amaryllis bulbs are a favorite around Christmas, but these statuesque beauties are having their seaons extended each year because of their immense popularity as a long-lasting cut flower as well as an interesting indoor bulb. Here these winter white amaryllis have been arranged with leafless Japanese magnolia into a glass vase filled with floral foam concealed by sand and delicate coral fern.

color concepts

There are dozens of reasons why I feel so lucky to have enjoyed a career working with flowers, but by far the single most joyful experience has been working each day with this immense choice and variety of color. Color is my inspiration, and it has a very powerful psychological effect on our state of mind. The color of nature is simply about attracting the attention of birds, insects, and animals for the pollination and fertilization of the plant kingdom. This very essential and sensual process in the plant world has always led to a close association between the natural plant color and human activity and has been an extremely enriching bond.

I think it is fair to say that some florists and flower arrangers have a very natural flair for using color and have an almost instinctual understanding of it. For many others, the use of color and the immense choice at their disposal is daunting, so it is necessary to have some basis of understanding of the theory of color. Over the next few pages, I outline some of the theory of color, although I have written more extensively about this subject in my seventh book, *Living Color*.

As a florist I understand the need to use color effectively to make an attractive arrangement and very often to convey a feeling or emotion on behalf of a client. Professional florists must work with the color preferences of their clients, and since most gift flowers are sent to convey an emotion, color plays an essential role in producing the desired result. When clients are ordering flowers, they more often talk of color thanvarieties of flowers or even their budget. Color is very often the first thing on our client's mind.

My favorite flowers—pink ranunculus—have been mixed with pink astrantia, rosy pink 'Sandy Femma' roses, and lime-green balls of *Asclepias physocarpa* 'Moby Dick'. Dyed pink coconut fiber and artificial butterflies give extra color to the overall flamboyant display.

Although white is not technically a color, more the absence of it, in the plant world it offers several color combinations. This living topiary is made of seven white amaryllis tied beneath their flower heads and at the base of their stems, arranged in a frosted glass vase with a collar of white lilac. The choice of a white container reinforces the monochromatic harmony of this design.

harmonious colors

A color harmony is created when a group of specific hues are placed together. There are three primary colors: red, yellow, and blue. By mixing them you create the secondary colors of green, violet, and orange. Intermediate colors are created when a primary and a secondary are mixed. The glaucous blue-green of the Savoy cabbage or hosta leaves is an intermediate color. The red-violet found in the dahlia and tulip families is another example of intermediate color. The twelve colors are known as hues, representing the names of the colors from which they were created: Yellow, yellow-green, green, blue-green, blue, blue-violet, violet, red-violet, red, red-orange, orange, and yellow-orange.

The intensity of color is the degree of saturation that the color projects. A fully saturated color, such as brilliant red, is more intense than maroon or burgundy. If you try to imagine colors in black and white, you can understand this further. A pale yellow is nearer to white, whereas a very dark brown is nearer to black. The perceived value of each color, how pure it looks, is relative to its position to black and white. Navy blue is lower in value because it is closer to black. Colors are lightened by the addition of white, muted by the addition of gray, and dulled by adding black.

Changing the value of a hue by adding white, gray, or black produces a tint, tone, or shade. By altering the value of a hue, an artist controls the effect or the emotion produced and stimulated. Mother Nature produces a diverse range of color, and it is the skill of the floral designer to combine this wonderful offering into a carefully orchestrated harmony of hues, tints, shades, and tones!

When one color is used to create harmony, it is known as monochromatic harmony. Often this produces the most subtle and pleasing of combinations and consists of a single hue in variations of tints, tones, and shades.

BELOW In true color theory, the use of green with red would not be considered a true monochromatic color harmony, but, since everything in the plant world includes some green, it is unavoidable in floristry color theory. Equisetum has been attached with double-sided tape and tied with sea grass to a glass tumbler into which a small posy of senecio, skimmia, 'Passion' roses, and red anemones have been placed.

RIGHT A hand-tied bouquet of deep red peonies, red skimmia, lime-green guelder rose, variegated deep red carnations, and stems of flowering rhubarb has been arranged into rings of rhubarb in this early summer arrangement.

BELOW Rosemary has been arranged around a glass tumbler onto double-sided tape and tied securely with sea grass, and a spring posy of ivy berries, senecio, narcissi, muscari, and pink ranunculus has been placed inside.

complementary colors

Using complementary colors is a good starting point for selecting flowers. They conform to our perceived thoughts on what good color combinations are, and this appeals to most people. Color in floral design has to be viewed from two perspectives. The first is the relationship of one color to another in the composition. This is expressed by the colors chosen and by their relationship in scale and size to one another in the design. To make a combination "look" complementary, you need to balance the colors fairly evenly. The second perspective is the relationship of color to the design. The colors must reinforce the design and the effect you wish to achieve.

A complementary color harmony is the combination of any two colors that lie directly across from one another on the color wheel. Green and red are opposite, and so are blue and orange, and purple and yellow.

These are known as complementary colors. When they are formed by using hues, either side of the color wheel, they are referred to as split complementary colors. Pale pink and lime green is one such split complementary color combination. The truest direct complementary combination on this page is the red and green, but because lime green is more of a hue, it also veers towards a split complementary. The pale pink, blue, and gray combination is visually complementary—although not strictly theoretically—because all the hues are very similar in their intensity. The color wheel theory is useful for an understanding of color and its relationship with other colors, but you will find that it soon becomes quite instinctual as to what works well and looks good and what jars the eye and is not so pleasing.

Cut limes conceal floral foam into which pink bouvardia, white lilac, pink calla lilies, pink 'Beauty by Oger' roses, and pink cymbidium orchids on a base of *Viburnum tinus* and ivy berry foliage have been arranged. Flowering *Viburnum tinus* has been used for the base, with some lime-green balls of guelder rose to carry the lime green of the fruited base through the pink arrangement.

This brightly colored ring of yellow and pink mixed with purple is essentially an analogous color combination. The pink and yellow gerberas have been interspersed with groups of 'Grand Prix' roses, orange leucospermums, purple double lisianthus, and the short-stemmed gloriosa. Fitted onto a pinholder in the center are five tall red heliconias.

mixed colors

Any color can be made to work with another color provided it is in the right balance and has the correct amount of foliage to create a foil for the color and texture. Being confident in mixing colors comes with experience, and each new season brings new hybrids and fresh color combinations with which to experiment. In nature, many different color mixes totally defy any serious "color theory," often within the same flower or plant! A clutch of multicolored wild flowers can often inspire an idea for a color scheme that I may not have considered. Sometimes an individual variety can suggest a new color scheme. A good color combination enhances the beauty of the

individual flower by placing it with other colors. Creams and whites are very enhanced by lime greens. Yellow can be best in a monochromatic design, but I like to mix it with blue, which sits opposite on the color wheel and therefore makes it a split complementary color, but I think it needs a lot of softening with foliage and texture to stop it looking too "corporate." Cobalt blue delphiniums work very well next to huge late summer sunflowers with tall yellow eremurus, some pale yellow 'Concordia' lilies, and a bunch of purple tracheliums and lisianthus. Soften it with some feathery yellow 'Dille' and you have a favorite yellow and blue combination.

BELOW Galax leaves have been used to line the inside of a stemmed glass bowl, which has then been filled with soaked foam and a bed of asparagus foliage. Forget-me-nots, soft blue lilac, lime-green guelder roses, deep purple anemones, hot pink gloriosa, and 'Milano' roses make this an analogous harmony of different colors.

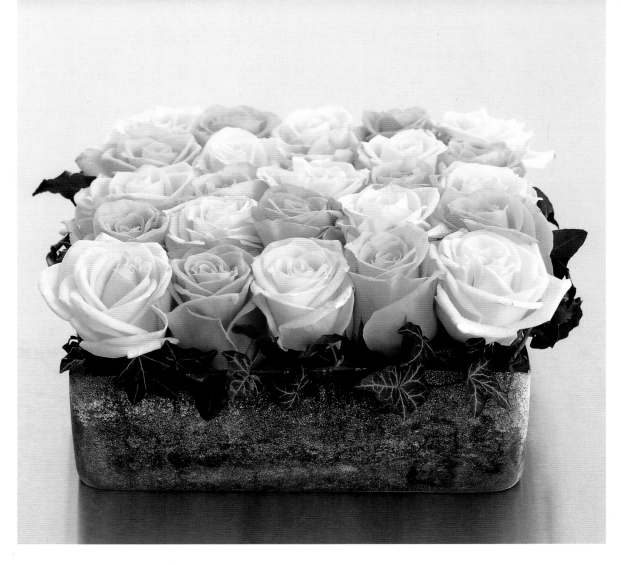

analogous colors

Colors that are on either side of each other on the color wheel are known as analogous colors. Generally speaking, this is one of the most popular and acceptable ways of mixing colors, and I have to say that it crops up time and again in my own work. I do not think about them as being analogous colors, but if I were to look back over most of the mixed colored arrangements in my portfolios, the vast majority would fit into this category with the addition of greenery! Not all my arrangements, however, would fit into the strict "color theory" definition, which states that an analogous color

combination should include one primary or secondary color with adjacent colors on the color wheel from a 90-degree angle. This is partly due to the constant addition of greenery, whatever the color combination.

An analogous color combination would suggests that they should be related. For example, yellow, yellow-orange, and orange work well, as do red, red-violet, and violet, and so on around the color wheel. In most flower arrangements, there is also the addition of the secondary color green, provided by the foliage, as a base for the color.

This analogous color combination takes in the lime, which is a yellow-green next to yellow on the color wheel and, on the other side, yellow-orange. A plastic bowl is covered in double-sided tape and encircled with yellow broom into which two blocks of floral foam are added with a chunky arrangement of cream 'Alexis' roses, 'Yellow dot' spray roses, guelder rose, 'Daily Star' green chrysanthemums, white skimmia, and some mixed sunflowers.

contrasting colors

Contrast is the difference shown when a variety of plant material is placed next to one other. As well as contrasting color, texture and form are important in creating a good arrangement; and whatever colors are chosen, they will both play an important part in achieving the overall look. Creating a good contrasting arrangement involves using the two colors on the outside of an analogous color mix in greater balance to those inside the semicircle. For example, blue and yellow are at the opposite ends of an analogous combination, so a more arresting color combination comes from having more of the two primary colors and less of the dark green in the center. It is the same with orange and green: they are at the ends of another analogous combination, so by using them without primary yellow in the middle, you get a more striking combination.

Complementary colors that lie across from each other can often make the strongest contrast, and if you use two colors that are too close to one another, you need to use texture to get a greater contrast. For example, strong textural contrasts are often needed to make monochromatic designs work.

BELOW Stripes of bright orange and lime green aquarium aggregate have been used to line a block of soaked floral foam in this 6-inch cube. Matching orange 'Wow' roses, bright orange germini gerberas, and textural orange leucospermum have been contrasted with green ivy berries, 'Lemon and Lime' roses, and 'Jade' hypericum.

Lilac hydrangea flowerets have been placed in a vase with layers of cellophane to create an iced water effect. A hand-tied bouquet consists of 'Daily Star' lime-green chrysanthemums, 'Green planet' roses, lilac hydrangea heads, guelder rose, *Alchemilla mollis*, and 'Duchess de Nemo' roses. Lime green is a very special color, and I use it a lot to create a fresh and more vivid color scheme, in a variety of combinations.

the effect of foliage

I use foliage to make colors tone together. Generally, I try to use at least three different types of foliage as that gives the finished design a more natural appearance. If you use the same group of flowers but add three types of foliage, usually with one in blossom or with berries, depending on the season, you will get a much better-looking design than if you choose just one type of foliage.

To make a combination brighter, add more lime green; to tone it down, use darker green, glossy foliage. To perk color up, lighten it by using foliage with more white, such the silver grays of eucalyptus or senecio. For more depth, use foliage with more black in the color—denser greens like huckleberry,

camellia, ruscus, ivy, and aspidistra. Brown foliage adds depth; photina, leucadendron, and cotinus with their lovely deep colors have more impact because of the contrast of the dark against the brightness of the flowers, so I often include these with my more unusual color combinations.

Green is generally a neutral color, but lime green is the least neutral, adding zing and vitality to any arrangement. Traditional flower arrangers have long lusted after lime-green foliage such as moluccella, *Alchemilla mollis*, hellebores, euphorbias, and hydrangea. The hybridizers know lime green is popular, and each season brings lots of new varieties to add to the collection of old favorites.

Although some variegated foliage can be great for flower arranging—such as pittosporum and varieties of eleagnus, holly and ivy—I am very wary of variegation as it can introduce a lot of yellow or cream and detract from the other colors. I therefore only use variegated foliages in winter when there is less choice, and I mix them with other evergreen foliages.

ABOVE This chunky bouquet of burgundy cotinus, lime-green leucadendron, pinkish peach rose 'Toscani,' green 'Baubles' South African foliage, *Berzelia galpinii*, and gardenia foliage is edged with anthurium.

LEFT A soft trailing wedding bouquet needs light foliage, whereas a bold design needs dense foliage for structure and balance. Here 'Toscani' roses are mixed with *Asparagus densiflorus* 'Sprengeri,' *Asparagus setaceus* 'Plumosus,' *Clematis montana*, and 'Gracia' spray roses.

LEFT White ranunculus and white parrot tulips have been mixed with glossy dark green foliage, ivy berries, and aspidistra for a sophisticated hand-tied arrangement.

BELOW Using a lighter green selection of foliage, which here includes the white flowering skimmia, *Alchemilla mollis*, and 'Jade' hypericum, gives the flowers a much more vibrant hue and overall a lighter visual effect.

part two

lessons

To be a successful florist and to forge your own style, you must first learn the basics, and then it is essential to get lots of practical experience. It takes time to become a competent florist, and a lot of this expertise is learned on the job. Throughout this section, each lesson is broken down to teach you the basics of flower arranging and floristry. Starting with mastering a hand-tied bouquet, the lessons then progress to making arrangements in foam, and using a pinholder, chicken wire, and even moss. Each stage is photographed to help you master the techniques and concepts required for arranging flowers in my style. Whether you are a veteran of the design workroom or new to the world of flowers, there is always something new to learn and new trends and fashions to keep your work fresh and appealing.

essential equipment

In the floral industry, the word "mechanics" is given to describe the equipment necessary to keep the flowers in place. To start off with, you only really need a good pair of scissors, a sharp knife, and some strong pruning shears. Next you will want to get hold of some wired string, and some blocks of floral foam and pot tape with which to secure the floral foam. Changes in commercial floristry have meant a greater diversity of media is now being used with flowers, such as shells, fruits, vegetables, gravel, and glass products such as donuts and test tubes, to name just a few.

You can buy floral sundries from either flower clubs or from sundries wholesalers. Most of these are attached to fresh flower markets. Some suppliers also sell these goods over the internet. Buy yourself a sturdy workbox and gradually build up your sundries as you perfect your skills.

ABOVE Floral foam was invented by Vernon Smithers in the United States, and one of the best-known brands is Oasis, from which it takes its common name. It can be purchased in many different forms, sizes, and recently in different colors. The green foam is for fresh stems and the brown, which is slightly denser, is intended for use with artificial and dried flowers. Apart from the standard block, there are jumbo blocks, cones, spheres, and many frames for the sympathy trade.

LEFT Some useful sundries: a roll of bindwire; a roll of floral tape; a roll of floral tac; a roll of double-sided tape; a hank of raffia and seagrass; a selection of wires; some pearl-headed pins; a roll of gutta-percha tape.

ABOVE Some of the most essential tools to my designs that I keep in my workbox are a choice of good knives to strip, clean, and condition the flowers. While I admit that a knife gives you a better cut, personally I prefer to use a strong pair of floristry scissors. A strong pair of spring-loaded shears are also very useful when dealing with different strengths of foliage and tough flower stems.

flower care

nomenclature of flowers

The floral designer quickly needs to learn the names of the plants that are available for his or her art. From my own experience, I found that looking for their individual costs on invoices so that I could price plant materials quickly speeded up my knowledge of the flower and plant world, and I was focused on learning the myriad of flowers and foliage available.

Most plants have popular names that vary with the country and from region to region. Generally, however, we use the botanical names, which allows us to exchange information internationally in the world flower market. Latin or Greek is used to describe the plant world, and our current system of nomenclature was devised by Karl Linnaeus, a Swedish botanist who lived in the eighteenth century.

This binomial system consists of two words. The first refers to the genus, which is a group of closely related plants to which the plant belongs, and the second is the specific species name. Often a certain hybrid may have more than one species, and each cultivar will have a cultivated variety, which is given single quotation marks. For example, beautiful scented sweet peas are called *Lathyrus odoratus*, and then each specific variety will have a specific epithet, so that one variety of lilac sweet peas will be called *Lathyrus odoratus* 'Lilac Ripple' where a burgundy and white bicolor will be *Lathyrus odoratus* 'Wiltshire Ripple.'

The international cut-flower trade is lucrative, and each year large sums are invested in increasing the assortment. This means there is a constant search for new cultivars and crossbreeding hybrids to produce new cultivars. Scientific research also plays a crucial role in improving the vase life of flowers and increasing the strength of flowers so that they travel farther. Since floral design has now become so immersed with interior design and the fashion world, there has been much more emphasis on trying to predict new trends so that the growers can be one step ahead of demand. The result is that each year the flower assortment becomes larger and the cut flower is a product very much in motion. Varieties come and go, new flowers and foliage become the rage while those with a poor vase life or who lose their popularity disappear from the scene. Sometimes they are flowers that are loved and enjoyed by customers, but because of their unreliability as plants—either they are prone to disease or have an unpredictable yield—they are therefore not profitable enough for the growers.

Every time a new variety is developed, the cultivar names fall under the International Code for the Nomenclature for Cultivated Plants. This is the committee that determines the names of plants, and sometimes when they are in dispute they determine new names. For example, the official generic name of the arum lily is now *Zantedeschia*. The former name was *Calla*, and that is often still used. For several years the florist's chrysanthemum was reclassified and given the Latin name of *Dendranthema*, but recently it has been restored to its original Latin name of *Chrysanthemum*. This kind of crossover of names is sometimes very confusing and daunting to the new student of floral art, but in a very short time you will astound yourself with how many new flower and plant names you have learned and are confident about.

when to buy

Generally speaking, most of the growers are very good and responsible at presenting their product to the market when it is at the right stage of maturity. Sometimes, however, flowers are cut too early and are not ripe enough or strong enough to flower. There are no hard and fast rules about this because the correct stage for harvesting varies enormously from one species and even among cultivars. Unripe flowers often contain fewer sugars and so as a result they absorb water less well and perform disappointedly. From my own experience, it is more likely that there will be unripe flowers available at peak times when the demand is high and the flowers have not quite reached maturity, or when flowers are in short supply and the demand is high, such as the wintertime. Generally speaking, most flowers are cut when the bud is showing good color, although some, such as gerberas, are sold when fully out. Also very occasionally flowers may have been cool-stored for too long, and the buds fail to open. Lilies are particularly prone to this, and it often happens around peak periods, such as Christmas and Valentine's Day, when the sheer demand for products puts too much pressure on the suppliers.

vase life

The value of a cut flower is often perceived by the general public by its longevity or "vase life." I have often heard delighted consumers raving about a certain variety because it has last nearly three weeks. Personally I find I am emotionally most attracted to the short-lived, often scented varieties, but both in my work and also in my home, I too am often drawn to the more practical long-lasting varieties. Once cut from the plant, flowers and foliages begin to age and will eventually wilt and die. This is of course a totally natural and irreversible process, although much research is expended into hybridizing varieties that last longer and looking for substances that will prolong the life of cut flowers, from feeding them food and antibacterial agents to giving them hormones or even Viagra to keep them holding up longer! The immense importance of the flower industry to the Dutch economy has resulted in most of the research on the factors influencing the longevity of and keeping properties of cut flowers being carried out in the Netherlands, and they have the authoritative position in the world.

conditioning

The term "conditioning" is the name given to the task of preparing the flowers on arrival from the grower or wholesaler for floral design or for sale as cut flowers. You need to recut the stems of all flowers and foliages and place them into a clean container. As a general rule, I would recommend taking ½ inch off the end of the stem, creating a slanted cut allowing the end of the stem to be exposed to the maximum surface area of water. Also remove any foliage from the stem that will be in water as this will cause bacteria to grow. And the less leaf on the stem, the easier it is for the flower to take up water to the all-important flower head. Also it is essential to make sure that the container and the water are clean and free from bacteria. Dirty water may be absorbed into the stem of the flower, but it will clog up the vessels within the stems and may then obstruct proper absorption of water by the flower and cause the flower to wilt prematurely. Flowers should never go into water that is too cold as lukewarm water provides more oxygen and is better for the longevity of the flower. Alkaline tap water holds more oxygen than slightly acidic rainwater. There are many nutrient-rich flower foods that can be added to the water that help clean and feed the flower. Some of these are available to the end users, and some more specific products are only used by the floral trade and the growers. When you receive your flowers, it is a good idea to condition them for several hours since many flowers may have had a very long journey between their grower to the end user, and they need to revive before being used for floral design. During the initial "condition" or drink, the flowers will take

up water rapidly, so generally deep water is recommended. All flowers start to pollute their own vase water as they age, and some varieties such as the narcissus family are worse than others. It is therefore beneficial if you can change the water often and refresh it with new flower food. There has been a long-established myth among flower arrangers, particularly in the United Kingdom, that it helps the flower to take up water more freely if the stem is cut up vertically in two, or if the ends of woody stems, such as lilac or *Viburnum opulus* (guelder rose), are bashed with a wooden mallet. There is absolutely NO scientific evidence for this, and in fact, all trials on longevity in flowers come out heavily against it. Bashing or cutting the flower ends destroys the valuable cell structure in the stem, which causes rot and bacteria, which in turn obstructs water absorption. So although this has widely been believed to be beneficial for a long time, it is in fact a myth and makes it much harder for the flower to absorb the water up the stem to the important flower head.

temperature

Room temperature is critical to the longevity of the flowers. Most flowers such as tulips and roses will last considerably longer at 50°F than they will at 70°F. Generally speaking, high temperatures and direct sunlight will cause a flower to mature quickly and shorten the vase life. Temperatures between 40°F and 50°F increase the life of nearly all flower varieties, however there are one or two exceptions, such as tropical flowers and the *Euphorbia* family, who prefer temperature over 60°F. If tropical flowers are kept in refrigerated conditions, they very quickly turn black and deteriorate.

evaporation

Cut flowers also need an equilibrium between the water they absorb and the evaporation from the plant. Flower shops are very humid places, and very often you will notice that a full flower shop has steamed-up windows as the natural process continues after the flowers have been cut from their plant source. Generally speaking, the growers try to take the flower to market in water so it can continue to absorb water. However, very often they will be removed from water for transportation to their end user. At this point many flowers and plants lose between 10 and 20 percent of their weight by evaporation, and however well conditioned when they arrive, they will never be restored to their former glory. If the flower has withered completely, there is nothing that can be done to revive it. The speedy transportation of flowers is therefore crucial to the success of the industry. Traders limit evaporation by wrapping the flowers tightly in paper and packing them in boxes. Keeping transportation cool and placing the flowers into water as soon as possible also helps.

Evaporation can also be limited by removing as much of the lower leaf from the stem of each flower, particularly with flowers where there is a lot of lower leaf, such as helianthus, celosia, roses, and chrysanthemums.

feeding cut flowers

Plants absorb energy from light by means of their chlorophyll, which is their green coloring matter, and store it in the form of sugar. The energy within the plant is broken down and used to create the growth and the life cycle for each plant. Once the flower or branch has been cut from the plant, the flowers do not have enough energy to breathe further. This energy shortage can be enhanced by feeding the cut flowers with sugars. Many flowers are fed a post-harvest solution to assist them on their onward journey from the grower to the end user. Many of these solutions contain sugars such as glucose to feed the flower and a disinfectant to prevent bacteria from growing. This explains why some of the household remedies for keeping flowers, such as adding bleach or sugar to the water, have accrued some credence.

Flower food helps to maintain the vase life of flowers. They are more likely to retain a better petal color, and the foliage should hold up better. The flowers are able to retain more energy, and the buds and flowers are helped to develop to their full potential. The flowers are less sensitive to damage from the aging hormone ethylene, which increases their longevity. Hormones created by the plant have a great influence on the life process. One of them, the aging hormone ethylene gas, influences the life of cut flowers unfavorably. This gas is produced by all plants; some of the gas remains in the plant, but some is released into the surrounding air. This aging hormone is also created by other vegetation, particularly ripening fruits and vegetables, and air pollution also increases the yields of ethylene. The more ethylene in the room, the quicker the flower is likely to die. Although I like to use a lot of fruits and vegetables in my designs, I generally restrict their use to event work or for special occasions when the display is not required to last, because they will shorten the life of the flowers.

Paula's top five tips

1 Check the maturity of the flowers that you are purchasing and unwrap them as soon as you can.
2 Cut the end of the stems obliquely using a sharp knife or a pair of scissors. Remove any foliage that will fall under the water line and any that does not enhance the ornamental value of the flower.
3 Clean buckets with a professional bucket cleaner or household bleach and disinfectant. Then add clean lukewarm tap water with flower food. Be sure to add the correct ratio of flower food to the quantity of water used.
4 Place the flowers in well-ventilated storage area, preferably at around 43°F and keep an eye on the water level, because the flower will drink a third of its water in the first twelve hours after it is placed back in water after its long journey from the grower.
5 Remove any damaged leaves or flowers and make sure you do not store flowers in proximity to any fruits and vegetables. Also avoid exhaust fumes and cigarette smoke, which can be harmful.

One stem of *Dianthus*
'Rosa Monica,' a standard
pink carnation.

flower conditioning

longevity of flowers
Not all cut flowers live for the same length of time. Most varieties live at least five days, some between eight and ten, and others will last up to three weeks. The success of a flower is often measured by its vase life, and there are many factors that determine how long a flower may live. The most common determining factor is the variety. Fragile, dainty garden flowers generally do not last as long as florist-bred flowers such as chrysanthemums, carnations, and tropical varieties. Scented varieties also generally do not last as long because a lot of their energy is expended in being fragrant. Many of my favorite perfumed flowers fall into this category, such as sweet peas, tuberosa, jasmine, lily of the valley, and stock. The second major factor is the length of time it takes for the flower to make the journey from the grower to the end user. If the flower has been post-harvest treated and kept in water, it will have suffered less trauma than a flower that has been harvested in South America, sent by air, dry packed to Aalseer in the Netherlands for auction, and then repacked and sent on to North America. Such a flower may have had a minimum of four days without water. In Europe, the proximity to the large flower auction in the Netherlands and the use of road transportation means that a lot of flowers are able to travel in water. This means that they are less traumatized and quite simply fresher when they arrive, and it makes conditioning far easier. In certain parts of the world where air transportation is the norm, the conditioning process can seem more like a "revival" process, as the flowers have been dry packed for a long time. It may mean that in those areas, certain flowers such as delphiniums and sweet peas have to be sourced locally because they are not good travelers, or they will rarely be used in floral design.

guaranteed life
The importance of how long a flower may live will vary according its purpose. For retail, gift, or contract flowers, the maximum life is of prime concern, but for special occasions, the flower needs to be in its peak condition to look its best. For sympathy work, weddings, and parties, the flowers need to be open and showy, making the ordering and storing of flowers a very vital role in any flower business. Many of the new retailers of flowers are happy to guarantee the life of their flowers in the same way they date stamp their fresh foods. I can testify that many of their claims are greatly exaggerated, as I have trialed many for consumer research, and at the end of the day, each of us has a different opinion on when a bunch of flowers is ready for the trash! I believe a reasonable expectation for a gift bouquet or arrangement should be five days. In my own company, we honor this with our customers and take care to make sure they are given the correct conditioning and maintenance advice in order to get the best from their flowers. Just as there are no guarantees on how long any of us will live, the plant world can be very fragile and unpredictable.

flowers from the garden
If you cut your own flowers, it is best to do this in the evening or first thing in the morning. The evening is my preference: at the end of the day the maximum reserves of food are stored in the plant. You can cut your plant material and leave it to drink water and flower food overnight—flowers and foliage will be strong and ready for arranging in the morning.

special tips for certain flowers

Anemone Remember that these flowers, which are available throughout the year except midsummer, are very thirsty drinkers, so fill up the vase well. Also it is important to consider that they continue to grow in water so bear this in mind when placing them in arrangements or hand-tied bouquets.

Anthurium These flowers, which originate from South America, and other tropical flowers such as heliconias from warmer climates, do not like the cold, and their optimum storage temperature is 65°F. They turn black if they are kept in temperatures below 60°F. They are generally packed into plastic and stored in boxes to protect them from cold and drafts in transit. They also are very susceptible to the natural salt found on human skin, so avoid handling them—this can result in black decolorization. These are long-lasting flowers—some varieties can last over fifty days—so it is less essential to use flower food with these varieties, but it does not do any harm.

Bouvardia This is a very delicate and pretty flower that is most useful for the bridal trade and delicate arrangements. It is extremely sensitive to dehydration, so it is best transported in water. If it is left out of water for a long time, it is very hard, if not impossible, to revive this fragile flower. It is a thirsty flower and requires deep water and the water level to be checked daily. Usually it is packed and sold by the grower with its own bouvardia flower food, which improves vase life. If the weather is cold, halve the normal dose to avoid leaf burn. This special bouvardia food will not harm other varieties. The best storage temperature is 40°–50°F.

Euphorbia This is a very big family, and there are many varieties that are popular within the flower trade. All euphorbias bleed when their stems are cut, exuding a milky latex substance that is an irritant to skin and can cause inflammation if placed near the eyes. Make sure you wash your hands thoroughly if you handle these flowers. You can simply cut the ends of the stems and condition in the normal way, but if you wish to use these flowers in a glass vase, you may want to seal the ends. The best way to do this is to plunge them into boiling water for five seconds. While you are doing this, try to protect the flower heads from the effects of the steam by wrapping them in paper.

Carnation Buy standard carnations when they are still firm and not too wide open. Spray carnations should show good color, and the most mature flower should be open. Micro-carnations should be bought when the flower is at least half open. Carnations have nodes along their stems, and the stems are thicker here. When conditioning or arranging, cut the stem between nodes to allow water to penetrate the stem.

Gerbera These brightly colored daisy flowers are post-harvest treated and then packed into cardboard boxes. They should be conditioned by cutting the end of their stems and then placing them in water while protecting the flower head. Usually this is done by hanging the flowers into a bucket while their heads are kept flat in their traveling cardboard "rack." This enables you to maintain a straight stem and also a well-placed head. Some growers protect the petals by placing them in a plastic ruff that sits at the top of the stem. In some countries, they are wired at the wholesale market, and many florists wire gerberas externally to keep them upright. If they are fresh, they should not need wire, and I would only wire them if my design required it or if I was planning to use them in bridal work. Try to avoid touching the flower head as this may cause damage, and

One weeping stem of *Euphorbia fulgens* 'Red Surprise.'

One hollow stem of *Hippeastrum* 'Mont Blanc' filled with a bamboo cane to support the flower head.

after the initial conditioning, do not place them in deep water. They have delicate hairy stems that can become limp and mushy if kept in deep water for a long time.

Helianthus These happy flowers are sensitive to dehydration, so do not allow them to dry out completely as they are impossible to revive. The flower is prized, but the foliage can be quite unattractive so it is a good idea to remove it. Their thick-stemmed flowers are very thirsty, so make sure you put them in very deep water when you first condition them. They are very sensitive to bacteria and so benefit greatly from flower food. Make sure that the vase you put them in is scrupulously clean and avoid earthenware vases, in which bacteria can multiply in the pores of the earthenware surface.

Hippeastrum These elegant flowers are sold packed into boxes. They have cavernous, long, hollow stems. The best way to condition them is to take off about an inch from the end of the stem and then insert a bamboo stake into the stem to protect the head while the stem takes water to the flower head. Most amaryllis have four heads, and they take over a week to open fully. These flowers have been heavily hybridized, so the head is very large and the stake in the hollow stem helps to protect the stem when the flower is fully extended. This also helps to protect them from "committing suicide" when placed in water over the edge of a glass vase, and also helps when using them in foam and intricate designs. The ends can split and become slimy, so try to recut the stems every two or three days or even use some tape if visible or florist tape if not visible around the bottom to protect the end.

Hyacinth This wonderful scented spring bulb is usually cut just above the bulb, and it is vital to the strength of the stems to try to keep as much of the base on

One fleshy stem of *Hyacinthus orientalis* 'Blue Jacket.' The white bulbous part on the stem will help to support the flower head.

One woody stem of *Syringa vulgaris* 'Hugo Koster.'

the stem as possible. Cut the minimum off the end, trying to keep as much of the woody, white stem to help support the stem when all the little fragrant flowerets have opened fully. Hyacinth bulbs are often cultivated in sandy soils so rinse off any grains before using the flowers.

Iris When you buy iris, make sure they are showing good color for at least an inch because if they are too immature, the buds will not open. Iris are short-living flowers, and they are very susceptible to bacteria, particularly botrytis, which is a fungus that grows on flowers. It is essential to dispose of these flowers if they are past their best as they can infect other flowers. Although I adore flag iris and grow many varieties in my garden, I only tend to use the commercial iris on its own, massed together where you can also appreciate its long, elegant stem. Its short life and star shape make it difficult to use with other flower heads.

Lathyrus Sweet peas are sensitive to dehydration, so they are often wrapped in water to keep them moist. Immediately recut the stems and place in no more than two inches of water. Try not to bunch them too tightly together or crowd them in a bucket, as they are very sensitive to botrytis. They naturally generate heat and can quickly start to wilt if they are massed together.

Lilium Lilies can often be cut too early or cold-stored for too long so that they never reach their full potential. Make sure that a few buds are fully developed and that some are showing the color of the flower. Look carefully at the bud to see that it is not unnaturally withered and also make sure that the foliage is lovely and green before you purchase. Although the anthers look lovely, they pollinate and can ruin the face of the flower as well as stain furniture and clothes, so pinch off the anthers from the end of the filament. This does not damage the flower. If any pollen does get onto clothes, try to remove it with tape and do not wet.

Matthiola This gorgeous scented flower, commonly known as stocks, is another short-lived beaut. Prized for its wonderful scent, like all fragrant flower it expends a lot of its energy in its scent to the detriment of its life. It is also very sensitive to dehydration and should not be left to dry out. As a member of the Brassica family, it can have a pungent smell if the water gets contaminated, so it is essential to use flower food. As it is very sensitive to bacteria, make sure the vase is scrupulously clean and avoid earthenware vessels, which have pores in which the bacteria can multiply.

Narcissus Although you can buy daffodils in tight bud showing no color, it is essential to purchase the multiple-headed narcissus such as 'Paperwhite,' 'Ziva,' or 'Churchill' when they are fully developed and loose. If they are cut too immature, they do not form fully and can be very disappointing. All narcissus produce slime that can be damaging to other flowers. It is essential to condition them for at least twenty-four hours before mixing them with other flowers, and it is best to use narcissus flower food that has been specially developed to neutralize the effects of the slime.

Nerines Nerines should also be showing color and at least one bud should be loose when you purchase them. These elegant flowers do not like temperature below 35°F and are generally very long-lasting flowers that are grown for the trade all through the year, but are in greater supply for the last five months of the year.

Orchids There are a huge variety of orchids, which generally require no special conditioning and are extremely long lasting. They are usually packed in water vials to keep them happy during transit, so on arrival recut the stems and place in water with flower food. They are sensitive to temperature below 60°F and really hate drafts. The more delicate phalenopsis orchid can be refreshed by submerging in lukewarm water if they have become flaccid.

Papaver Sadly most poppies are short lived, both in their natural habitat and also as cut flowers. *Papaver nudicaule* last between six and nine days. Most poppies are supplied with their stems singed because they exude a milky sap. If you need to trim the stems, it is essential that you resinge them with a naked flame. Oriental and somniferum varieties generally last about four days, but they are useful to a florist for their seed head, which can be used green or dried in long-lasting arrangements or Christmas decorations. The seed head is tremendously long lasting.

Paeonia Peonies are gorgeous seasonal flowers, which are susceptible to bacteria and benefit enormously from flower food. To help open tight buds, spray occasionally with water, which helps to dissolve the sugars that can prevent the buds from opening fully. They are very sensitive to temperature fluctuations so keep them in a cool spot.

Rosa Roses should be purchased when the bud is fully developed and showing color with fresh leaves. Flower food is essential. Recut stems frequently and refresh often for maximum vase life. Remove thorns and lower foliage with a sharp knife without damaging the stem.

Tulip Tulips should be purchased when the bud is fully developed and showing color. The foliage should show no disease. If the tulips are droopy, which happens to the more heavily hybridized varieties, such as parrot or double tulips, recut, wrap them in paper, and place in a cold spot for several hours so they can straighten up. Tulips continue to grow in a vase, and it is important to remember this if mixing them with other flowers.

One hairy singed stem of *Papaver nudicaule*.

One woody stem of Rosa 'Coolwater.'

hand-tied flowers

A hand-tied bouquet is simply a bunch of flowers and foliage that has been spiraled in the hand and then tied at the binding point ready to be placed into a vase. It can often be aqua packed (wrapped with water) so that it makes the perfect gift. It takes most people a few attempts to get the hang of this, but after five or six attempts it soon becomes quite instinctual! It is certainly the design I use the most and is one of the most versatile arrangements. Mastering the skill of the hand-tied is central to creating many of my trademark designs. When I started my business nearly twenty years ago, the hand-tied bouquet was very popular in continental Europe, but scarcely seen in the United Kingdom. In the last fifteen years it has become very popular here and is now gaining popularity all around the world. It is most regularly used as a gift item to take to someone's home or to have delivered by a florist. However, its uses have now become so widespread that everyone who loves to arrange flowers wants to learn this skill to create contemporary vase arrangements for their own home. Looser, flat-backed versions can be used as swags or chair backs for Christmas displays or weddings, and sleek small versions can be used as bridal bouquets or bridesmaids' posies. Tightly packed bouquets can be used to top vases for a more formal look in corporate or event work.

When you are selecting the materials for a hand-tied arrangement, I recommend that you start with a bunch of straight and strong flowers such as a bunch of roses. You need at least twenty stems to make a bunch, and twenty-five to thirty-five is the average. Thoroughly clean the lower stems to make them free of thorns and foliage. It is impossible if there is greenery at the binding point, as the bunch becomes difficult to handle, and it is then hard to achieve a good spiral. In any case, you need to keep the stems nice and clean so that when you put the flowers back in water there is no greenery in the vase to prematurely age the bouquet.

An early summer hand-tied bouquet mixes the spring flowers of lilac, guelder roses, anemone, and ranunculus with summer peonies.

simple hand-tied bouquet

This simple hand-tied bouquet of vibrantly colored roses is the best way to practice your hand-tying technique. The flowers are straight and sturdy, and they are one of the easiest to use. A mass of the same flower is easier than a mix of different flowers and foliages. I like to edge this design with folded aspidistra leaves, which are inexpensive and make for a very fetching contemporary bouquet. One round of leaves is very effective, but you can continue to several rounds to accentuate the massed roses within.

materials
20 stems of *Rosa* 'Ruby Red'
20 stems of *Rosa* 'Coolwater'
20 stems of *Rosa* 'Milano'
15 stems of aspidistra leaves
a roll of cellotwist
a roll of ribbon
a sharp knife
a roll of pot tape

step by step

1 First, strip all the foliage from the stems; working from the top to the bottom of the stem, prize off the leaves and thorns with a sharp knife.

2 Taking the central rose in your left hand (if you are right-handed, vice versa if you are left-handed), place the next rose to the left of the first at an angle of around 25 degrees. Place the third one just left of that until you have a fan of seven stems. At this point, start to turn them by taking your other hand and twisting them about a half turn. Next add another five stems in exactly the same manner and then twist again.

3 Keep adding roses in this pattern until you have a nice round dome of roses. Tie tightly with floral cellotwist at the binding point where you have been holding the roses.

4 Loop the aspidistra leaf by placing a small piece of pot tape around the stem. The leaf will last well like this as the stem is still in water. Edge the bouquet with the folded aspidistra leaves. Finally make a 3-loop ribbon bow and tie it around the stems.

grouped bouquet

Putting flowers in groups allows you to use more striking color combinations than when you mix them all up. It allows you to experiment with both colors and the textural element of the plant material. Grouping flowers is currently very fashionable and makes any design look more contemporary.

materials
5 stems of *Rosa* 'Sphinx'
5 stems of *Viburnum opulus* 'Roseum'
5 stems of *Hyacinthus orientalis* 'Blue Star'
10 stems of *Anemone coronaria* 'Mona Lisa Blue'
3 stems of *Rosa* 'Wow'
3 stems of *Rosa* 'Sunbeam'
3 stems of *Hydrangea* 'Challenge Blue'
a stem of *Chrysanthemum* 'Shamrock'
a bunch of *Narcissus grootkronige* 'Cheerfulness'
3 stems of *Rosa* 'Grand prix'
a bunch of *Ranunculus* 'Ranobelle Inra'
a bunch of coral fern (*Gleichenia polypodiodes*)
a bunch of *Hedera helix*
5 stems of *Hypericum inodorum* 'King Flair'
a roll of floral bind wire

step by step

1 Taking a central group of three 'Sphinx' roses, start to build up your grouped hand-tied by placing plant material at a 30-degree angle to the left of the previous placement. Every three or so placements twist the bouquet in your hand so that you are working on all sides and creating a spiral posy. Add bunches of foliage throughout to create a more textural effect.

2 Continue building up the tied bunch so that you have a good mix of color throughout, and as you continue, the plant placements will be at a 45-degree angle to create a nice rounded shape. Edge with the coral fern and tie at the binding point where you have been holding the flowers with floral bind wire.

Bind wire is a floral product created especially to tie spiraled boquets firmly. It has a central wire covered by paper so that it gives a tight tie without damaging any of the more delicate stems. Trim the ends of the bouquet so the flowers fit neatly into the vase and top up with water and flower food.

tropical bouquet

This hand-tied bouquet is often also known as a limited design or a line bouquet. The principle of adding the flowers is the same as with a hand-tied round bouquet except that you are keeping the back flatter and the final design will be essentially front facing or it will have one side more attractive than the other. I use this design when more architectural flowers are chosen, and very often when the customer requires a more masculine bouquet. In this design, there are two distinct areas of interest: the striking shape of the heliconias with the willow; and the denser lower area filled with textural flowers and foliage.

materials

5 stems of *Heliconia stricta* 'Huber'
5 stems of *Leucospermum cordiolium* ' Sunrise'
1 thick stem of date palm (*Phoenix roebelenii*)
5 *Monstera ldeliciosa* leaves
5 branches of contorted willow (*Salix matsudana tortuosa*)
5 stems of *Bixa orellana*
a bunch of *Cordyline fructicosa* 'Negri' leaves
several lengths of raffia
a roll of Japanese paper

step by step

1 First remove all the lower foliage from the flowers and lay them out in bunches already arranged. Take one piece of willow and place one heliconia slightly to the left of the willow at an angle of 25 degrees.

2 Add the rest of the willow and the tall heliconias at the same angles to the left and right of the central flowers. Next arrange a group of the leucospermums to the left of the bouquet.

3 Add the rest of the plant material in groups allowing the date palm the central position so that it can trail over the front. Edge the bouquet with monstera leaves and then tie with raffia.

4 Fold a length of Japanese paper and place around the binding point. Create a bow from several lengths of raffia by making two loops and then tie through the center to create a figure eight. Add to the biding point to secure the paper.

bouquet in a vase

The overwhelming majority of my designs are made in glass vases because they allow you to create a very sculptural design by placing different plant material or media in the vase. This particular design was inspired by the discovery of a new treatment for roses where this large 'Avalanche' rose has been dipped in a special solution of paint to create a flocked effect, which ironically makes a natural rose look almost like a fabric flower.

materials

1 large clear glass urn
with a frosted plinth
1 frosted vase
a length of floral bind wire
a pair of scissors
1 bag of marshmallows
a bunch of *Viburnum tinus*
a bunch of *Camellia japonica*
a bunch of *Ranunculus*
'Cappucino Pink'
10 stems of *Rosa* 'Marshmallow'
10 stems of *Tulipa* 'First Class'
12 stems of *Rosa* 'Barbie'

step by step

1 Fill the bottom of the urn with marshmallows. Place the frosted glass vase into the center and stuff the sides with marshmallows.

2 Taking a central 'Marshmallow' rose and a piece of foliage, start placing plant material to the left of the central rose at an angle of about 25 degrees.

3 Add a sprig of *Viburnum tinus*, a ranunculus, a 'Barbie' rose, and a tulip, all slightly to the left of the piece before. At this point you need to turn it in your hand, so take your right hand and twist it.

4 Place the flowers and foliage at the same angle. Continue adding and twisting every five or six pieces of plant material. The stems should start to fan out, and you can start to see the spiraled stem of the posy.

5 Continue until you have used all the plant material. As the bunch starts to grow, the flowers and foliage will be placed at more of a 45-degree angle. Using the floral bind wire, bind and tie tightly where you have been holding the bunch. Trim all the stems with a diagonal cut; if the bouquet is well balanced, it will stand on its own stems.

6 Fill the central vase with water and place the bouquet in the center of the vase. Gently recut the binding point so that the flowers loosen up a little bit and just fall over the edge of the vase.

wrapped bouquet

Round bouquets can be wrapped in a number of ways. The most common wrapping is cellophane, which can also be used to aquapack the flowers so they are delivered in water. The wrapping helps to protect the flowers as well as making them more decorative. We also use tissue and Japanese papers, as well as fabric and Deconet to enhance our gift bouquets. Fileted banana leaves make a lovely natural biodegradable foil for floral bouquets and are a favorite of ours for rose bouquets for Valentine's Day.

materials

10 stems of *Tulipa* 'Winterberg'
10 stems of cream *Ranunculus asiaticus*
5 stems of cream *Hyacinthus orientalis* 'City of Harlem'
7 stems of *Rosa* 'Alexis'
5 stems of *Viburnum opulus* 'Roseum'
5 stems of *Skimmia japonica* 'Fructo Alba'
3 stems of berried *Hedera helix*
a roll of bind wire
a roll of cream Deconet
a roll of cellophane
a length of ribbon

step by step

1 Carefully remove any foliage from the lower stems of all the flowers. Arrange your materials in groups and begin to make the spiral bouquet by taking one central flower and placing plant material slightly at an angle to the left of the first central flower. This may start at an angle of around 30 degrees, and as you get to the end of the bouquet may be more like 45 degrees. Continue doing this with the three other stems and then twist the bunch around in your hand and add another five stems to the left. Continue twisting the bouquet every five pieces of plant material so you are working on all sides. Remember to continue to use pieces of foliage throughout the bouquet to help create structure and add interest to the bouquet.

2 When you have added all the plant material, tie with the bind wire at the point where you have been holding the bouquet. Cut a piece of thick cellophane and place it around the base of the stems to create a bag for water. Tie the cellophane securely and fill the bag with water.

3 Cut a length of Deconet to go around the bouquet and tie around the middle with a 3-looped bow.

LEFT Try this selection for an alternative bouquet:
7 stems of *Gloriosa rothschildiana*
10 stems of *Rosa* 'Milano'
10 stems of *Rosa* 'Supergreen'
7 yellow *Zantedeschia aethiopia* 'Florex Gold'
10 stems of *Hypericum* 'Brown Flair'
7 stems of *Chrysanthemum* 'Shamrock'
½ bunch of bear grass (*Xerophyllum tenax*)
10 stems of hard *Ruscus hypophyllum*

wedding posy

For over a decade, the round hand-tied posy has been the most popular design for wedding celebrations. Generally we do not cover the stems since many brides prefer the natural "just picked" look and rarely do we cover the stems of the attendant's posies. When requested to cover the stems with ribbon or fabric, we often use double-sided tape.

materials

7 stems of 'Sarah Bernhardt' peonies
10 stems of pink *Astilbe* 'Erika'
10 stems of *Alchemilla mollis*
10 stems of pale pink sweet peas
10 stems of bicolor pink *Rosa* 'Carnival'
a length of bind wire
a roll of pot tape
a roll of double-sided carpet tape
a roll of matching ribbon
a pair of ribbon scissors
a sharp knife

1

2

3

step by step

CLOCKWISE FROM TOP RIGHT The finished step-by-step wedding posy; a bridal bouquet of white 'Akito' roses hand-tied with *Bouvardia* 'Diamond White;' a posy of 'Vendella' roses, pink rancunulus, blue muscari, and *Bouvardia* 'Diamond Pink;' and two bridesmaids' posies of pink ranunculus edged with galax leaves.

1 Strip all the lower foliage off the ends of the stems and clean the thorns off the roses by using the edge of a sharp knife. When they are ready, place each variety in piles so that you can mix up the varieties as you begin to spiral your posy. Start with a central rose, then add a stem of *Alchemilla mollis* at a 25-degree angle and then a stem of *Astillbe* to the left of that at the same angle and a sweet pea in the same way. After that you will need to start to twist it in your hand so you are working on all sides of the design.

2 Continue adding five or so stems and then twisting the bouquet until you have achieved a lovely spiral-stemmed bouquet. Tie with bind wire at the point you have been holding the bouquet, which is known as the binding point.

3 Starting at the binding point, tape together the spiraled stems with pot tape, working down to the bottom of the handle.

4 Next add two strips of double-sided tape down either side of the taped handle. Take a roll of ribbon and, starting from the top, bind around the handle by diagonal loops until you reach the bottom and then bind all the way up to the top again.

5 Cut off the additional ribbon at the binding point of the bouquet and then make a bow from three loops of ribbon with one central tie. Fasten the ribbon to the binding point with the bow.

4

5

victorian posy

Flowers of concentric circles are often known as Victorian posies and are sometimes referred to in North America as Biedermeier designs. The word Biedermeier actually refers to a period of furniture design, painting, and literature in Germany and Austria during the period from 1815 to 1848. Concentric circle arrangements were also the height of fashion at that time in Victorian England. These tightly packed rings of the same type of flowers are sometimes wired, but more often are hand tied. This delightful posy is a modern take on an old idea with its structural ring of fresh spring contorted willow.

materials

20 stems of *Tulipa* 'Winterberg'
1 stem of *Rosa* 'Alexis'
25 stems of *Narcissus tazetta* 'Avalanche'
5 stems of *Salix babylonica* 'Tortuosa'
50 stems of *Muscari botryoides* 'Album'
50 stems of *Frittillaria meleagaris*
a roll of bind wire
a roll of floral tape
a length of heavy wires
a pair of scissors
a roll of ribbons

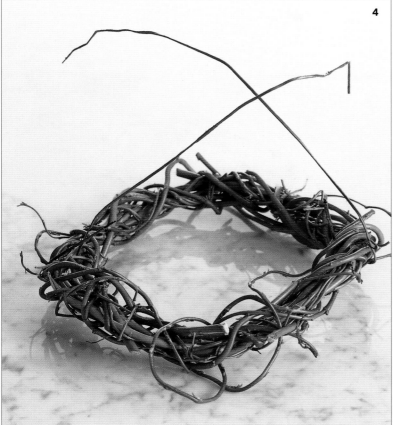

step by step

1 Choose a good specimen of 'Alexis' rose for the center of the bouquet and then place bunches of five stems of white muscari all the way around the rose. Tie with bind wire at the binding point to secure the flowers.

2 Working slightly farther down from the muscari, add a ring of the narcissi to be the same width as the muscari. Secure again with bind wire.

3 Add a row of tulips. Secure them with bind wire. This massing of heads where it overlaps is sometimes referred to as a pave (see page 60).

4 Twist the five stems of contorted willow into a small wreath that will fit snugly around the posy. Tape with floral tape two heavy wires and secure them into either side of the ring.

5 Complete the posy by adding bunches of the frittillaria around the posy. Place the wreath ring around the base of the flower heads and secure by placing the two taped wires through the center of the posy. Finally trim the ends of the posy and add a 3-looped bow.

This ballerina bouquet includes *Matthiola incana* 'Francesca,' *Zantedeschia vivalda*, variegated hedera helix, *Lupinus* 'Little Eugenie,' astilbe japonica europa, solomon's seal, *Syringa vulgaris* 'Dark Kosta' and *Rosa* 'Prima Donna.'

ballerina bouquet

This bouquet is designed for presentations on stage. It is a formal style of arm bouquet where the flowers are arranged as a teardrop with an extension of the stems showing for the recipient to hold. Usually carried in the fold of the arm, this style of bouquet can be used for weddings, where it is known as an over-arm bouquet, but is more often requested for the stage in Europe. In North America, where it is called a presentation bouquet, it is also often used for beauty pageants. In London, I arrange them for divas of the opera or much more commonly for ballerinas performing at the Royal Opera House or the Coliseum.

materials

5 stems of *Gloriosa rothschildiana*
10 stems of *Lupinus* 'Terracotta'
10 stems of *Matthiola incana* 'Francesca'
10 stems of *Viburnum opulus* 'Roseum'
7 stems of double lilac *Eustoma russellianum* 'Mariachi Misty Blue'
10 stems of *Panicum* 'Fountain'
10 stems of solomon's seal (*Polygonatum multiflorum*)
10 stems of *Amaranthus cordatus*
a roll of floral bind wire
a pair of scissors
a roll of organza ribbon
a sharp knife

step by step

1 Clean all the lower foliage from the stems of the flowers and plants. Using a knife, prize off the thorns from the roses to reveal straight and clean stems. Taking some of the trailing foliage, begin the bouquet using the solomon's seal, amaranthus, and *Viburnum opulus*.

2 Continue to build up the bouquet, adding the flowers as you go along, taking each variety and placing it in a zigzag across the center of the design.

3 You are aiming to make a diamond-shaped outline with a profile that is triangular with the highest point in the center of the bouquet and tailing down to the binding point. Add any of the fillers, such as the fountain grass, into any of the gaps you have and then tie with the floral bind wire.

4 Trim with a bow by making three loops of ribbon and tying another length through the center.

CLOCKWISE FROM TOP LEFT: Silver rope napkin tie, using white skimmia, green 'Jade' hypericum, and starring the white 'White Revert' chrysanthemum. Pink napkin with floral tie of senecio, flowering eucalyptus, 'Milano' rose, pink hydrangea, and wire-edged pink ribbon. Beautiful scented gardenia heads with leaves, wired onto the napkin with wire embellished pearls. Three gloriosa flower heads tied with a silk-wired cord.

materials

1 small plastic water vial
1 laurel leaf
a length of raffia
3 stems of *Hedera helix*
a branch of *Viburnum tinus*
5 heads of *Helleborus orientalis*
a pair of scissors

napkin rings

Floral napkin ties can be a lavish touch to a large formal celebration or a rather personal, simple touch for a dinner party. For formal events, I often do a ribboned bow and a flower for each guest, or on some occasions, just for the female guests. Little posies placed on each napkin can be a more personal way of decorating the table than creating single or even several centerpieces.

step by step

1 First wash the ivy and leave to dry. Place two stems of trailing ivy around a napkin, twisting it over itself so that it stays in place.

2 Fill up the vial with water and cover with a laurel leaf tied with raffia. Arrange your flower heads into to a little diamond-shaped posy. Cut the ends of the stems neatly and place into the vial. Tuck the water vial into the twisted stems of trailing ivy.

chair backs

A floral chair back has become very popular for weddings and can be used for both formal and informal occasions. Most often a chair back is a tied sheaf of flowers. One of the reasons for the growth in popularity is the huge diversity of venues that are now licensed to hold weddings. A row of chair backs enhances an aisle for a ceremony or marks out the top table in situations where the bride and groom have chosen to have a round table instead of more formal long, one-sided top table. Very often we move them from the ceremony to the reception so they get to be used throughout the wedding day. They are usually attached to the side for an aisle and centrally placed on the chair for a top table. The choice of flowers can make them look formal or informal. The use of one type of flower such as the hydrangea creates a more contemporary look.

materials

5 stems of *Gloriosa rothschildiana*
5 stems of *Helianthus annus*
'Sunrich Orange'
5 stems of *Rosa* 'Milano'
3 stems of *Viburnum opulus* 'Roseum'
3 stems of yellow *genista*
½ bunch of berried *Hedera helix*
7 stems of *Asparagus umbellatus*
1 bunch of *Skimmia japonica* 'Rubella'
5 stems of *camellia*
a roll of bind wire
a roll of ribbon

step by step

1 Find one piece of flat foliage to use as the base for this hand-tied. Build up the foliage to create a triangle using some flat foliage and some trailing foliage.

2 Continue adding bushy foliage such as the skimmia and ivy berries to improve the profile of the chair back. The highest point of the foliage should be above the point where you are holding it.

3 Begin to arrange your flowers by loosening your hand and threading your flowers through the foliage and into the desired place. Start at the end and, working on alternate sides, place each variety of flowers through the design to the base. Finally place the roses and sunflowers across the design and add some extra foliage at the binding point to trail over the front. Tie with bind wire.

4 Attach to the chair with ribbon.

OPPOSITE TOP LEFT
One perfect stem of white *Hydrangea macrophylla* 'Schneeball' make a modern decoration for this classic chair.

OPPOSITE TOP RIGHT
Trailing ivy and berried ivy have been wired to create a garland across the top of the chair which then has had *Eustoma russellianum* 'Echo Pure White,' cream 'Gracia' spray rose, *Lathyrus odoratus, Rosmarinus officinalis,* and ranunculus wired into it.

OPPOSITE BOTTOM LEFT
A hand-tied bunch of margarite daisies (*Argyranthemum frutescens*) with a natural raffia bow.

OPPOSITE BOTTOM RIGHT
A floral lei of white Singaporian dendrobium orchids have been strung together on a heavy transparent thread.

arrangements

Strictly speaking, an arrangement is defined as plant material in a container. This actually would include many of my hand-tied bouquets because once they are placed into a container, they become an arrangement. However, in our flower school here in London we first teach students the art of hand tying and then move onto arranging. For an arrangement, the starting point is usually the container. Arrangements come in many forms and can be small or large vase arrangements with no mechanics. They can also be huge urns and trailing mantelpieces with sturdy mechanics to keep the flowers in place and the arrangement well balanced. By far the most commonly used mechanics for arranging flowers is the green foam sometimes known by its brand name Oasis. For larger arrangements or for delicate flowers such as muscari or heavy-stemmed flowers such as hyacinths, chicken wire is preferable because it allows the flowers to drink more freely. Grids of tape, wires, pinholders, gel, and even cellophane and moss are all examples of the mechanics used to anchor and support flowers, as well as natural products such as twigs, shells, and stones.

The style and shape of an arrangement is determined by its destination and purpose. A table arrangement may be low and small enough to fit the table and allow the seated guests to see and talk to one another, or it may be so vast and impressive that it has one or two tiers and the guests sit under the design. For corporate arrangements and weekly contract work, one of the main concerns is that the flowers last well, so here the emphasis is on choosing reliable plants that all look good together and last around the same amount of time.

A tall glass vase filled with jalapeno peppers, and topped with contorted willow, *Physallis alkekengi* 'Jumbo,' and orange *Euphorbia fulgens* 'Sunstream.'

securing flowers

Green foam is more commonly known by its major brand Oasis. The accidental discovery of this compound in North America, which absorbs water and is principally used to hold the flowers in place and provide them with a source of vital water for their longevity, radically changed the way flowers could be arranged and particularly delivered. It is largely responsible for the creation of less naturalistic trends in floristry from the 1960s on when it became more commonly used.

floral foam spheres

materials

30–35 mixed mini gerberas in monochromatic colors
a teardrop-shaped vase approx. 8 inches in height
a 4-inch green floral foam sphere

Spherical foam balls are available in a number of sizes and are useful for creating pomanders, topiary, or massed round designs. Balls can either be impaled on a stick or vase to create a standard topiary form or they can be hung. Small hanging decorations are usually suspended from a ribbon and are often created for bridesmaids. Large spherical arrangements are created by wiring together two hanging baskets filled with floral foam and covered with 1-inch chicken wire. A decoration of this size is often used to hang in large halls or party tents.

step by step

1 Soak the floral foam until the air bubbles cease to rise. Press it hard down onto the ridge of the vase so that it is firmly balanced.

2 Starting from the base, work up to the top to cover one-half of the ball with the mini gerberas (sometimes known as germini) heads. Trim the stems about an inch long to avoid breaking up the floral foam too much.

3 Continue with the other half of the ball until there is no longer any floral foam visible.

floral foam ring

Round floral foam rings are made in a multitude of widths. The large 14- and 16-inch wreath frames are very useful for large table centers for round 4- or 6-foot banquet tables. Into the center you can place bowls or storm lanterns filled with candles. Often we group flowers together to create a very colorful table center; here we have used the flowers in a very natural way, grouping some flowers but using the length of others to give the arrangement movement and rhythm.

materials

5 stems of sunflower (*Helianthus annus* 'Orit')
1 bunch of green *Rancunculus* 'Clooney'
10 stems of *Rudbeckia hirta*
a bunch of white flowering *Skimmia confusa* 'Kew Green'
a bunch of *Genista tinctoria* 'Royal Gold"
7 stems of *Zantedeschia aethiopica* 'Best Gold'
a bunch of chanel *Mimosa acacia crassa*
3 bunches of *Galax erceolata*
a bunch of flexi grass (*Xanthorrhoea australis*)
a bunch of pussy willow (*Salix caprea*)
7 *Anthurium crystallinum* leaves
a 6-inch round wreath frame
9 floating candles
a straight-sided glass bowl

step by step

1 Soak the floral ring until the bubbles cease to rise. Trim the top of the corners of the oasis to make it easier to put the plant material in. Edge around the ring with galax leaves, taking care to cover the plastic base.

2 Place groups of foliage at different heights and depths along the ring, starting with the skimmia, then the flowering genista, and then create loops encircling the ring using stems of the flexi grass.

3 Place stems of pussy willow in the oasis by putting the stem end in and then the other end in so that they are orbiting the ring. Place the seven anthurium leaves in the oasis so they are all pointing the same counterclockwise way. Then place groups of rudbeckia, ranunculus, and sunflowers into the ring.

4 To complete the rhythm of the ring, place the ends of the stems of the calla lilies in the foam and twist them under the willow so that they follow the counterclockwise movement of the design. Finally add sprigs of the mimosa around the ring to fill any gaps.

5 Place a glass bowl in the center of the ring. Fill with water and floating candles.

using colored floral foam

There are two main types of floral foam; green, which is absorbent for fresh flowers, and brown, which is denser and created for dried or artificial flowers. Recently a number of different colors of floral foam have been created. It is semiabsorbent and can be used for fresh flowers or dried or artificial flowers. I use colored floral foam when creating fruit bowls.

materials

I block of orange floral foam
5 oranges
9 stems of *Rosa* 'Milva'
9 stems of *Rosa* 'Wow'
30 stems of *Rosa* 'Milano'
10 stems of *Germini* 'Aisha' (mini gerbera)
7 stems of *Leucospurmum cordifolum* 'Tango'
a bunch of *Calendula officianalis*
'Greenheart Orange'
15 stems of *Gloriosa rothschildiana*
8 stems of *Celosia cristata* 'Bombay Pink'
7 stems of *Viburnum opulus* 'Roseum'
a bunch of *Camellia japonica*
a bunch of ivy berries (*Hedera helix*)
20 stems of *Ruscus hypophyllum*
a tall-stemmed lead glass fruit bowl
a length of pot tape

step by step

1 Soak the floral foam in water and then place upright in the center of the container. Meanwhile cut slices of orange just under ½-inch thick and place around the edge of the bowl. Using a thin strip of pot tape, tape the foam securely in the bowl. Trim off the corner of the floral foam to make it easier to put the plant material in at all angles.

2 Taking the three types of foliage, establish the outline of your arrangement and completely cover the floral foam before adding any flowers. The colored floral foam requires slightly more and denser foliage than green foam.

3 Next add the thick-stemmed flowers such as celosia and the woody-stemmed flowers such as the *Leucospurmum* and *Viburnum opulus*. Next add the roses in groups and then the marigolds and mini germini.

4 Finally add the delicate flower heads of the *Gloriosa rothschildiana* and top up the water in the bowl, together with added flower food.

fixing with tape

materials
16–20 bunches of *Muscari*
175 bunches of flexi grass
(*Xanthorrhoea australis*)
a roll of tape
(thin green floral tape
is best, but thin clear
tape will work as well)

Grids of tape like this are very useful for shallow glass containers where green floral foam would be inappropriate or difficult to use. I usually use grids for low glass bowls, particularly crystal glass. Here I also chose to use a grid of tape rather than floral foam because the massed stems of muscari would have been almost impossible to pack so densely into foam and they will survive better with more access to water. The tape holds the bunches of flowers in place while allowing them to drink the water freely.

step by step

1 Line the glass dish with swirls of flexi grass so that it fits snugly around the edge. Using single lengths of floral or clear tape make lines of one way and then across the other to create a grid of tape with holes of around ¾-inch square.

2 Fill with water mixed with flower food, which will keep the water clean and free from bacteria. This is very important when you are using plant material such as the flexi grass below the water line. Working from one side of the bowl, place small bunches of muscari into each square until you have covered the whole grid.

using a pinholder

materials

20 stems of *Allium*
'Purple Sensation'
a glass dish
a 2-inch flower pinholder
a roll of 'Floraltac' adhesive

for the base

40 stems of *Tulipa* 'Blue Diamond'
18 stems of *Hyacinthus orientalis*
'Minos'
24 stems of *Rosa* 'Blue Pacific'
12 stems of *Viburnum opulus*
'Roseum'
24 stems of *Rosa* 'Green Planet'
40 baby eggplants
40 stems of *Skimmia laureola*
12 branches of *Senecio greyii*
a bunch of coral fern (*Gleichenia
polypodiodes*)
10 stems of *Ruscus hypophyllum*
an 18-inch floral foam wreath frame
a length of heavy wire

Pinholders are very useful for anchoring a few flowers into a low container. They are used mostly for minimal flower designs or for ikebana. I tend to use them for tall, architectural flowers such as members of the allium, iris, strelitzia, helleconia, and agapanthus families.

step by step

1 "Floraltac" is a waterproof clay that has been designed especially for the floral industry to secure and anchor objects into an arrangement. Take an inch of floral tac clay and rub it together in your hands to make it warm. This makes it more adhesive. Place it in the center of the dish and push the pinholder down on the adhesive clay until it is firm.

2 Cut the ends of the alliums and impale them on the pinholder, making sure they are all the same height. Start in the center of the pinholder and work to the outside until the pinholder is completely covered.

3 Soak the wreath frame in a large bucket until the air bubbles cease to rise. This should take about five minutes. Take care not to force the foam under water because this can create an air lock in the foam and then it does not retain the water. Cut the outside and the inside edge off the floral foam ring so you can line the edge of the frame with coral fern. Continue to cover the foam with groups of foliage. I have used gray senecio, white flowering skimmia, and dark green ruscus. Next, add the flowers in groups of odd numbers. Wire the eggplants by placing a heavy stub wire through the base and twisting the two legs together and then place them in the ring in large clumps.

containers

One aspect that made my work original was to use containers that were not intended for flower arranging, such as fruit bowls, plates, and dishes. This has now become such a trend that many companies specialize in making items just for the flower trade. Currently huge glass vases that contain the flower arrangement within are in vogue. Cube containers, minimal containers with an Eastern influence, and vessels made of zinc and metal also proved very popular. New trends emerge as changes in fashion and interior design come and go!

Wire baskets that can be filled with moss are one of my favorites for natural summer flowers. Here an urn and a basket shape have been filled with ivy, hypericum, senecio, skimmia, veronica, hebe, hydrangea, sweet pea, and 'Sterling silver' roses.

LEFT Two stems of vanda orchid have been arranged in a zinc moon vase with three stems of anthurium leaves, five stems of trailing weeping willow, and a handful of spanish moss.

BELOW As I am very attracted to brightly colored flowers, I am also interested in finding containers to accentuate this or to be very feminine. I sometimes cover vases in fabric or use little bags such as this beaded purse to contain the flowers. This simple arrangement is a more contemporary twist on the traditional basket arrangement. Ten stems of the pale pink rose 'Universe' have been hand tied and aqua packed and placed in a small sequined basket for a very feminine arrangement.

Rustic containers such as terra-cotta pots or oil jars from Provençe fashioned out of the earth always look good with flowers because they are natural and in empathy with the bouquet. They may not currently be as fashionable as they were, but for me, they are still items I return to each year. I also like wooden trugs and wire baskets for the same reason—they are classical and pleasing. If you are choosing a container for a few flowers, such as the beautiful vanda orchids pictured above, you need a strong vase design. A few flowers need a strong form, and this is why the container is such an intergral part of the design if you study oriental floristry such as Ikebana. The color and shape of the container are also vital considerations, and they should be in sympathy with the flower color and a suitable size for your chosen plant material.

Another important consideration when chosing a container is that it is sturdy enough to hold the mechanics and the flowers. Large arrangements that may use urns and pedestals need to be heavy or well weighted because the water and plant material will be very heavy and can easily be top-heavy if the base is not substantial. We use a lot of fiberglass urns and plinths for our weddings and also lacquerware, taking care to make sure the arrangements are well-balanced in the containers. For heavy fruit arrangements, you need to use heavy metal bases because the weight of the moss and fruit will be too substantial for weaker containers.

I personally prefer to customize my own container and make it part of the overall design. The arrangement then takes on a much more sculptural look, and your eye is not so

LEFT A heavy metal urn has been decorated with thirty wired oranges and camellia leaves placed into a cone of 1-inch chicken wire filled with spagnum moss.

OPPOSITE ABOVE
A tricolored dogwood arrangement in green, red, and black has been used to line a block of oasis in a 6-inch cube vase. Three rows of roses—'Black Baccara,' 'Jade,' and 'Grand Prix'— have been arranged in straight lines to pick up the theme of the stripes of dogwood.

LEFT A lightweight resin vase has been filled with kiwi vine to create a framework to arrange long stems of *Gloriosa rothschildiana*. The vase and arrangement have a natural empathy since they are both nearly see-through.

OPPOSITE BELOW A small cylinder vase has been filled with swirls of thin-stemmed Iranian dogwood and a hand-tied posy of 'Grand Prix' roses edged with galax leaves has been placed on the top.

drawn to the two elements, the vase and the container. For many years we have been covering inexpensive plastic containers with double-sided tape and natural greenery such as leaves or herbs like rosemary and lavender, which still works very well for table arrangements, especially when the client wants to keep the arrangement and does not want the expense of the vase.

However, in my own home and for the vast majority of arrangements, I prefer to use glass because it is so versatile and can be dressed up very easily with each passing season and be reused again and again. Here these two vases have both used the same plant material in two very different ways. The round swirls of the Iranian dogwood suit the petaled dome of 'Grand Prix' roses, while the lines of three-colored dogwood suit the geometric arrangement of the roses. Both containers are in empathy with the flower design and make up the overall effect.

small vases

I love to use small pots of flowers down a long table so you still have lots of room for large serving plates, and it gives you a chance to use delicate small flowers. It also looks more casual and contemporary than one large, long arrangement down the center.

materials
5 old glass French yogurt pots
40 stems of *Fritillaria olivieri*
50 stems of *Muscari armeniancum*
'Blue Spike'
10 stems of white *Rosa* 'Princess Spray'
50 stems of Lily of the Valley
(*Convallaria majalis*)
a length of Ivy leaves (*Hedera helix*)
a length of raffia
a pair of scissors

step by step

1 First tie two ivy leaves onto the sides of little yogurt pot glasses with a length of raffia.

2 Fill the pots with water mixed with flower food and then arrange little bunches of flower heads in your hand. Cut the spray roses up so you can use the individual heads. Trim the ends of each bunch to fit the pot.

large vase

If you are using a large glass vase, you can use the natural structure of the stems to anchor your arrangements. The vase should be more than half the height of the flowers so if your lilies are three feet long, I recommend a vase of twenty-four to thirty inches. The average length of flower sold is generally around twenty-four inches so it is a good idea to buy some containers ranging from seven to ten inches for arranging flowers at home.

materials
6 stems of *Prunus serrulata* 'Pink Cloud'
a 24-inch tall flared glass vase
7 stems of oriental dark pink *Lillium* 'Mero Star'

step by step

1 Fill the vase with water mixed with flower food. The flower food acts as an antibacterial agent as well as food for the flowers. It helps to keep the water clear and the flowers to have an enhanced life. First arrange the six branches of foliage in the vase, which will give you a structure into which you can then place the lilies.

2 Take all the lower foliage off the ends of the stems so they are clean. It is important not to have foliage in the water so that it does not cause bacteria buildup. Pinch out the pollen from the center of the lilies that are slightly open and add them to the vase.

one glass vase four ways

materials

a big tub of pink dried larkspur
a big tub of blue dried larkspur
a 6-inch cube glass vase
a larger U-shaped glass vase
a roll of floral bind wire
a pair of scissors
30 stems of *Tulipa* 'First Class'
30 stems of *Tulipa*
'Gander Rhapsody'
30 stems of *Tulipa* 'Synaeda Blue'

By far the most used vases in my collection are small cubes or tank vases, which I have in a number of sizes from four to eight inches. They are extremely versatile and can be used with an inner vase liner so that fruit, candy, and sand can be used, or filled with floral foam that is concealed from the outside by using leaves, reeds, and berries.

OPPOSITE TOP RIGHT
A glass cube arrangement, comprising of:
8 lemons
2 blocks of yellow oasis
half a bunch of ivy berries (*Hedera helix*)
5 stems of white *Skimmia confusa* 'Kew Green'
5 stems of *Hypericum* 'Jade'
3 stems of *Asclepia* 'Moby Dick'
9 stems of *Rosa* 'Supergreen'
12 stems of *Rosa* 'Alexis'

OPPOSITE BOTTOM RIGHT
To achieve this multicolored arrangement, you will need:
a large bag of jelly beans
a 6-inch glass cube with a tumbler packed inside
half a bunch of *Viburnum tinus* berries
5 stems of rosehips
5 stems of *Hypericum* 'Jade'
5 stems of white *Skimmia confusa* 'Kew Green'
5 stems of *Alchemilla mollis*
5 stems of *Rosa* 'Alexis'
5 stems of *Rosa* 'Supergreen'
5 stems of *Rosa* 'Milano'
5 stems of *Rosa* 'Beauty by Oger'
5 stems of *Rosa* 'Grand Prix'
5 stems of *Rosa* 'Milva'

OPPOSITE   This stunning tall arrangement would suit a large event. To make it, use:
a 6-inch cube and a 4½-inch cube
a bag of blue sand a bag of white sand
15 stems of *Agapanthus* 'Donau'
half a bunch of flowering *Eucalyptus perriniana*

step by step

1 Place a layer of pink larkspur blossom at the base of the u-shaped vase. Put the 6-inch cube on top of the blossom and then add a layer of dark blue blossom and then a layer of pink blossom and carry on in stripes until you reach the top. Fill the inner vase with water and flower food.

2 Strip all the tulips of their lower foliage and hand tie them into a spiral bunch by placing each stem at a 35-degree angle to the left of the previous one. Every five or six tulips, twist the bunch in your hand so that you are working on all sides.

3 Trim the tulip stems and place in the central glass vase filled with water and flower food. Gently cut the tie to relax the tulips so that they move over the edge of the container.

flat container

Flat- and straight-sided glass containers are among my favorites because they allow you to customize your container in so many ways. Here I have used blond mikado reeds, a dried reed grown principally in South Africa. We also use equisetum in the same ways, as well as other green reeds. Exotic leaves with great markings are also effective for this sort of treatment, as well as thinly cut slices of citrus fruits such as oranges, lemons, and limes.

materials
a bunch of dried blond mikado reed
(*Ischyrolepsis hystrix*)
4 stems of *Rosa* 'Black Baccarra'
8 stems of *Rosa* 'Bella Donna'
8 stems of *Rosa* 'Wow'
an oblong glass dish
a block of floral foam
a length of cord

step by step

1 Soak the floral foam until the bubbles cease to rise. Cut the floral foam to fill the base of the glass dish, leaving ½ inch around the edge. Cut the mikado reed to the same height as the glass dish to fill the gap between the edge and the foam. Cut the rose heads and place in the foam to create a neat line.

2 Continue across the dish with rows of different colored roses. It is important to try to choose roses that have heads of a similar size so that it creates a very graphic arrangement. Edge with four bundles of mikado reed tied with matching cord.

spring arrangement

Glass containers are extremely versatile and can be easily adapted to create many different designs. Two of my favorite liners for circular arrangements are dogwood and pussy willow. Both of these stems are very malleable in the spring when the sap is rising. These straight-sided bowls are very versatile because they can be used encased by floral foam as well as be decorated inside—see My Signature Style on page 23 or Color on page 74. A twelve-inch diameter bowl is my most popular.

see My Signature Style on page 23 or Color on page 74.

materials

20 stems of pussy willow
(*Salix caprea*)
5 stems of *Viburnum opulus*
'Roseum'
a bunch of *Camellia japonica*
5 stems of *Hyacinthus orientalis*
'Annalisa'
10 stems of *Veronica* 'Dark Martje'
5 stems of lilac (*Syringa vulgaris*
'Dark Koster')
10 stems of *Anemone coronaria*
'Mona Lisa Blue'
10 stems of *Ranunculus ranobelle*
'Inra Wit'
10 stems of *Tulipa* 'Negritta'
a bunch of *Senecio greyii*
a bunch of ivy (*Hedera helix*)
a 12-inch straight-sided glass bowl
2 blocks of floral foam

step by step

1 Wind the pussy willow around the inside edge of the glass dish. Place one block of soaked oasis in the center of the bowl and cut the other into two halves and place round the side so that it fits snugly, and the oasis is an inch or so above the edge of the glass container.

2 Green up the floral foam by using the small sprigs of the three varieties of the foliage, making sure they all radiate from the central point of the arrangement.

3 Next add the five stems of *Viburnum opulus* and lilac and then the more delicate spring flowers such as the hyacinths, tulips, and veronica.

4 Finally add the anemones, placing them at different heights and depths throughout the arrangement.

vegetative arrangement

Vegetative designs present floral material as they naturally grow so that the arrangement is mimicking nature. Very often in this style of arrangement, the plant material is placed in groups. Stem placements may be parallel (upright) or radial (fan shaped), with the stems arranged as they grow. If the flowers grow upright next to each other, as do liatris, gladioli, and antirrihinums, you would arrange them in that way to depict a vegetative or naturalistic design. If they bend out, such as irises or strelitzias, they would be arranged in a more radial position.

materials

10 stems of *Strelitzia reginae*
20 stems of contorted willow
50 stems of *Phormium tenax variegatum*
15 stems of *Leucospermum cordifolium* 'Coral'
10 stems of camellia
10 stems of lisianthus
10 stems of *Hypericum* 'Dolly Parton'
10 stems of *Rosa* `Macarena'
10 stems of *Eustoma russellianum* 'King Violet'
an 8-inch glass cube
2 blocks of floral foam
a length of floral foam tape

step by step

1 Lay out six stems of *Phormium tenax* horizontally and then weave another six stems vertically through to create a basketweave effect. If you find this difficult, you can always use a staple gun to keep the bottom and top leaves in place.

2 Trim to fit neatly into the glass cube. Use some floral foam tape to keep it upright until you are ready to add the oasis. Pack out the floral foam so that the container is completely filled and make sure that the foam is at least two inches above the edge of the container.

3 Add the willow throughout the arrangement and then green up the base with camellia followed by groups of leucospermums, roses, lisianthus, and hypericum. Finally add the strelitzia so that they are all pointing outward from the center of the arrangement.

creating a natural container

Using a plastic container, you can create lots of natural bases for table arrangements. I like to create my own containers because it gives the end result a more sculptural effect. It can also be a very inexpensive way of concealing a simple plastic pot if you use dark glossy leaves such as aspidistra, laurel, or rhododendron.

materials
1 pot of *Calluna Vulgaris* 'Silver Green'
5 branches of *Senecio greyii*
5 stems of *Hypericum* 'Jade'
6 stems of white *Chrysantheum* 'White Revert'
3 stems of *Brassica oleracea* 'White Crane''
3 stems of *Rosa* 'White Princess'
6 stems of *Rosa* 'Akito'
6 stems of *Rosa* 'Lemonade'
a branch of *Annus glutinosa*
3 stems of *Trachelium caeruleum* 'Lake Powell'
5 stems of *Garrya elliptica*
5 stems of *Hedera helix*
an 8-inch plastic bowl
a roll of double-sided tape
a 6 x 2-inch pillar candle
a roll of decorative florist wire
4 heavy florist stub wires or wooden skewers
a roll of florist tape
2 blocks of floral foam

step by step

1 Place a length of double-sided tape around the plastic pot. I prefer to use heavy-duty carpet tape from hardware stores. Cut little bunches of heather from the plant and stick them to the double-sided tape.

2 Bend the heavy florist wires into hairpins and tape onto the end of the candle.

3 To secure the heather, place a wire or a ribbon around the bowl. Fill the bowl with two blocks of soaked floral foam. Make sure that the foam is almost an inch above the edge of the container by packing out the bottom with the ends of the block of foam. Trim the bottom of the wires on the candle and then place firmly in the center of the foam so that the candle is well anchored.

4 Use the foliage to cover the floral foam, making sure that it all radiates from a central point. Use at least three different types of foliage to give an interesting textural effect.

5 Place the large-headed flowers into the arrangement at different heights and depths around the bowl. Next add the hypericum cut up into small sprigs. Use the roses in groups to balance with the larger, heavy flowers. Add the white *Chrysanthemum* 'White Revert.'

RIGHT A glass tumbler edged with laurel leaves and filled with a spring posy of hellebores, tulips, spray roses, skimmia, *Viburnum opulus*, and hyacinths.

BELOW RIGHT A basket externally lined with rosemary and blossom and filled with roses, ranunculus, lilac, and *Viburnum opulus*.

BELOW LEFT Cut rosemary edges a bowl filled with gloriosa, 'Milano' roses, yellow ranunculus, yellow and pink carnations, jade hypericum, leucospermum, and ivy berries.

creating organic containers

The combination of fruits and vegetables mixed with flowers has for a long time been popular with flower arrangers. I love to use capsicums, Savoy cabbages, melons, and pumpkins as containers scooped out and filled with foam, or attached around other containers with glue, wire, or double-sided tape in the case of asparagus, leeks, and sugarcane. Round vegetables such as radicchio, turnips, and eggplants work very well cut in half and scored so they fit on the edge of the bowl or wired around the container.

materials

10–15 globe artichokes
1 plastic pot
a length of aluminum wire
a roll of double-sided tape
a roll of pot tape
a block of floral foam
10 stems of green dill
5 stems of *Viburnum opulus* berries
a few stems of hebe
10 stems of dark dahlias
10 stems of *Rosa* 'Circus'
10 stems of red peonies

step by step

1 Cut the artichokes in half and clean out the choke. Thread onto aluminum wire until you have enough to go around the bowl. Tie the wire tightly around the bowl, twisting the ends.

2 Start placing your foliage into the arrangement, beginning with the hebe and followed by the viburnum berries to give a loose feel.

3 Place your roses throughout the arrangement, followed by the peonies, and fill in the gaps with the dahlias.

4 Complete the arrangement using the dill to achieve a soft finish.

ABOVE Three glass tumblers have been encircled by double-sided tape onto which I have attached spears of asparagus. Small posies of 'Cherry Brandy' roses, green 'Prado' carnations, *Alchemilla mollis*, and *Asclepias* posies have been added into the vegetative tumblers.

RIGHT Eggplants have been cut into half and scored to sit on the top of a straight-sided plastic bowl. Moss has been added to the gaps and the vegetables have been secured with raffia. In the center, floral foam has been added, and sprigs of *Viburnum tinus* blossom, and small bunches of black grapes have been wired with a double mount and placed around the arrangement, all radiating from the centerpoint. 'Nicole' and 'Aroma' roses have been placed in the arrangement with the brown 'Choco' mini gerberas.

basket arrangement

Baskets usually made from interwoven cane, rushes, wood, or metal are used throughout the floral industry. Round baskets and arrangements are perfect for centerpieces for tables and are also extremely popular as gifts. All baskets need to be lined with plastic to hold either floral foam or water and chicken wire. For this delicate spring collection of flowers, it is best to use chicken wire and water, as it allows all the fragile stems to drink more freely than they can in floral foam. Many of the spring bulbs such as hyacinths, muscari, and scillas, and fragile flowers, such as margarite daises and forget-me-nots, will last much longer if they are arranged in water rather than foam.

materials
a round gray basket
a round plastic pot
a length of chicken wire
a spool of florist wire
10 stems of *Tulipa* 'Blue Diamond'
5 stems of *Viburnum opulus*
'Roseum'
10 stems of *Scilla sibirica*
5 stems of lilac (*Syringa vulgaris*
'Dark Koster')
20 stems of *Myosotis*
10 stems of *Argyranthemum*
frutescens
a bunch of berried *Hedera helix*
a bunch of *Senecio greyii*

step by step

1 Fill the basket with a plastic liner and then add a foot of 2-inch chicken wire. Make sure that it fits snugly in the plastic pot and then attach with loops of wires to the basket so that it fits firmly. Fill the plastic container with water mixed with flower food.

2 For most of my designs, a third of the plant material will be foliage, and I usually like to select at least three different varieties to create a good base for the flowers. Start by adding the ivy, then the senecio, and then the lime-green blossom balls of the *Viburnum opulus*.

3 When the chicken wire is covered, you can begin to add the flowers. It is best to start with the woody stemmed flowers such as the flowering lilac and the heavy bulb stems such as the scillas.

4 Then add the tulips, taking care to make sure that all the stems radiate from the central point and that each flower is represented throughout the arrangement at different heights and depths to create a natural effect. Finally add the delicate flowers such as the daisies and the forget-me-nots.

larger arrangements

When creating an impressive arrangement, take time to secure your mechanics and make sure your chicken wire or foam is well wired and taped. Secure the bucket inside the urn or container. Use the foliage to establish the outline. Remember to recess some of the plant material so that it draws they eye into the design, and keep it topped up with water.

materials

a stand and amphora
10 stems of *Lillium* 'Sorbonne'
15 stems of *Paeonia* 'Red Charm'
10 stems of *Viburnum opulus* 'Roseum'
10 stems of flowering *Photina fraseri* 'Red Robin'
10 tall branches of *Sorbus aria* 'Majestica'
10 tall branches of *Prunus* 'Sato-zakura'
10 stems of *Antirrhinum majus* 'Potomac Rose'
5 stems of white *Delphinium elatum* 'Snow Queen Arrow'
15 stems of larkspur (*Delphinium consolida* 'Pink Perfection')
5 long branches of rhododendron
10 stems of long *Ruscus hypophyllium*
10 stems of lilac (*Syringa vulgaris* 'Dark Koster')
10 stems of weeping willow (*Salix babylonica*)
8 stems of solomon's seal (*Polygonatum*)
10 stems of *Moluccella laevis*

freestanding amphora

To create a really large arrangement, it is best to choose flowers of many different shapes. Tall flowers give the arrangement height while star-shaped and round flowers help to give the arrangement body. Around a third of the arrangement will be made up of foliage and to create a really natural effect, try to use at least five varieties. Pick some that are bushy, some that are tall, and some that are trailing. All the plant material should give the impression that it radiates from one central point; the stems will not all actually radiate from the same point as this would lead to an awful lot of crisscrossing at one point.

step by step

1 Line the pot with a plastic bucket. Use some scrunched-up chicken wire to allow the pot to sit flush with the container. Fill with water mixed with flower food.

2 Using a mixture of foliages, create the outline of the arrangement you wish to create. For a large freestanding arrangement, the flowers should be 1½ times the height of the container.

3 For a round arrangement, all the stems should radiate from a central point. Once you have a good base and structure with the foliage you can start to add the flowers, beginning with the prunus.

4 Use trailing foliages such as the ruscus, solomon's seal, and willow to trail down over the front of the pot.

5 Next add all the woody stems such as the lilac and the viburnum and all the tall spires such as moluccella, antirrhinum, larkspur, and delphinium.

6 Finally add the star-shaped lilies throughout the arrangement at different heights and depths and then place the peonies to fill any gaps.

trailing top-table arrangement

Trailing arrangements like this are useful for top-table arrangements, conference tables, or placing on mantelpieces. For a top table, I use a low spray tray but for a mantel arrangement, particularly if the mantel isn't very deep, I prefer to use a trough such as a windowbox so you can place the floral foam blocks upright. This gives you more potential for filling the container with water as well as allowing you to create a more substantial arrangement.

materials

10 stems of *Rosa* 'Vendella'
10 stems of *Rosa* 'Peach'
10 stem of peach spray rose
10 stems of *Lupinus* 'Little Eugenie'
10 stems of *Alchemilla mollis*
10 stems of *Panicum* 'Fountain'
10 stems of *Tulipa* 'Angelique'
7 stems of *Paeony lactiflora* 'Sorbet'
20 stems of *Polygonatum multiflorum*
10 stems of *Astilbe* 'Europa'
1 long spray tray
2 blocks of floral foam
a roll of floral tape

step by step

1 Soak the two blocks of floral foam in water until the bubbles cease rising and then place the two blocks on a flat white spray tray and tape them down. Trim the corner of the oasis to help the placing of the material. It is always best to make this kind of arrangement in situ, so place the tray right at the front of the table and start to create the outline by using the trailing stems of solomon's seal.

2 Next add the fountain grass evenly throughout the design.

3 Fill out the design by using the *Alchemilla mollis* and *Viburnum opulus* and then place seven of the lupines through the design as your longest flowers.

4 Using the spray roses and the standard roses, fill out the design and then place the open peonies in the most prominent positions. These central flowers will be the area that the eye is drawn to, which is known as the focal point.

5 Fill any gaps with the astilbe, working from the trailing edge through to the edge of the foam on the other side. Although these arrangements are often viewed from the front of the table, make sure it also looks good from the back which will be the view of the guests of honor and the people sitting at the top table.

oval table decoration

The heaviness of ivy foliage in this arrangement gives it a very natural feel and makes this an oval mass design. If you wish to create a more horizontal feel to your arrangement, use more stems parallel to the surface of the table. When the horizontal stems predominate, the arrangement is known as a horizontal design.

materials

1 bunch of white *Ranunculus* 'Ranobelle Inra Wit'
5 stems of *Syringa vulgaris* 'Madame Florent Stepman'
1 bunch of *Tulipa* 'Winterberg'
1 bunch of *Hamamelis virginiana*
7 stems of *Rosa* 'Alexis'
7 stems of *Rosa* 'Avalanche'
5 stems of *Viburnum opulus*
a bunch of ivy trails (*Hedera helix*)
a bunch of fruiting ivy
a 12-inch long rectangular container
a tall pillar candle
2 blocks of floral foam
a roll of floral tape
2 green bamboo skewers

step by step

1 Soak two blocks of floral foam and arrange in the rectangular container so the foam is at least an inch above the edge of the container. Cut the green bamboo skewers to create four legs and tape them to the bottom of the candle. Press the candle down in the center of the arrangement so it is firmly anchored.

2 Next take the ivy trails and help establish the flowing outline of the arrangement by using the longer pieces at either end of the arrangement. Use ivy berries to create a diamond-shaped base for your flowers.

3 Add branches of the witch hazel and the *Viburnum opulus* throughout the arrangement to create movement and to add interest.

4 Taking each individual flower, place through the center of the arrangement at different heights and depths using a zigzag motion from left to right. Fill in any gaps with sprigs of white lilac.

wirework

Traditionally speaking, wiring flowers was the preserve of the professional florist and separated them from the "flower arrangers" who tended only to make arrangements. Wiring is used to reinforce in a visually unobtrusive manner weak or fragile stems to support the flower heads or to create floral items to be worn or carried. Principally, flowers are wired either to be worn, for small- and large-scale decorative work, or for hanging. Before the widespread use of floral foam, wiring was much more prevalent because moss was primarily used, so it was necessary to wire flowers far more often. In fact, before foam wreath bases were invented, all floral sympathy tributes were made this way. There are still a few florists and nurserymen who make these tributes in the traditional way, but sadly this skill is dying. Wiring flowers obviously is more labor-intensive than arranging them in foam or hand tying, so it is more expensive and less economic.

The general rule for wiring is to use as light a wire as possible to do the job and then to keep it as neat as possible. Florist wire comes in many gauges and lengths, and you need to pick a wire to secure the flower or other plant material that is just strong enough and not so heavy as to damage the flower or stem, or make your work look too rigid and not natural enough. You have to be very careful also when handling the flower not to damage the petals by bruising, as this will quickly cause discoloration.

Wiring for weddings is generally delicate and somewhat complex and requires patience. Wiring for large-scale decoration or for the Christmas period is very hard on your hands and nails. Two more reasons why wiring flowers and plant materials does not suit all wannabe florists!

RIGHT Large heads of pink cymbidium have been wired into a posy, and the handle of wires has been covered with a matching silk ribbon.

boutonnieres

Boutonnieres are wired flowers with leaves that are designed to be worn on men's lapel. They are called "buttonholes" in Britain. Such a collection of flowers and leaves to be worn this way by a woman is called a corsage. Generally speaking, a boutonniere can be made from any type of flower, but there are some that are far more popular because they are inexpensive and wire well. Carnations and roses are particularly popular since they last very well; orchids are very successful, too, but tend to be more expensive to purchase, germini (small-flowered gerberas), mini-sunflowers, ranunculus, smaller calla lilies, and even daisies, cornflowers and stephanotis are among the flowers we are regularly asked for.

materials
a pearl-headed pin
3 sprigs of rosemary
a branch of *Viburnum tinus*
a stem of *Rosa* 'Alexis'
a branch of *Hedera helix*
a length of Parafilm
some 0.71mm wires
some 0.28mm or 0.32mm wires

CLOCKWISE FROM TOP LEFT Green cymbidium orchid edged with camellia leaves; Speckled phalaenopsis orchid with lily grass loops and camellia leaves; Carnation with lime hypericum; Hebe and gloriosa with grass loops, and a binding of decorative pink floral wire.

step by step

1 Select a well-formed rose and remove the stem just below the seedbox. Insert a short 0.71mm stub wire into the stem and up into the seedbox. Double-leg mount three sprigs of rosemary and two sprigs of *Viburnum tinus* flowers. To create a double leg mount, make a hairpin bend with the wire and loop one wire over the over three times. Choose three good ivy leaves and stitch through the vein at the back of the leaf and take one leg over the other.

2 Take a spool of Parafilm and stretch it to bind the wires together. This helps to keep the moisture in and softens the wires. Arrange three pieces of rosemary around the rose head and the two sprigs of *Viburnum tinus* berries and then edge with the three ivy leaves. Bind them all together with the Parafilm and then trim the stem so that it is just over an inch long. Add a pearl-headed pin so that the boutonniere can be secured onto clothing.

ABOVE Corsage of two cymbidium heads with jasmine and gardenia leaf. This is a beautiful combination, both long lasting and fragrant!

RIGHT A simple garland of margarite daisies threaded through their stem and the center of their flower head.

ABOVE For a last-minute touch for a wedding, you can wire flower garlands and heads onto a trug and add petals. Here we have used clematis, snakeshead fritillarias, and 'Aroma' rose petals.

RIGHT This bridesmaid's hoop has been simply bound with ivy and then covered with clematis and bunches of brodiaea and cornflowers. Wired heads of hydrangea have been added through the ring.

wired accessories

Wired accessories are generally made for celebrations, wedding in particular. Baskets and bridesmaids' rings are simply bound, and as fragile blooms have been used, they need to be made at the last minute and will only last for the duration of the ceremony. If you require wired flowers to last for the whole day, you

need to wire each indvidual flower head and leaf and choose long-lasting varieties such as roses, orchids, gypsophila, and good drying flowers such as lavender, eryngium, echinops, statice, limonium, and helichrysum. As an alternative, I would advocate last-minute wiring with simple binding wire as long as the bearer has been warned of the short life expectancy of the design. The napkin rings on these pages have been created by wiring flower heads onto either decorative florist wire or delicate silver wire.

materials

a reel of purple florist wire
a spool of ¼-inch ribbon
a stem of *Hyacinthus orientalis* 'Minos'

step by step

1 Pull the individual flowerets off the hyacinth and thread tham onto the length of purple wire so they all face the same direction.

2 When you have completed enough to bind the napkin, loop the two wires together and trim with a 3-looped ribbon bow.

bridal headdress

Wearing a ring of flowers dates from ancient Greece, and it is the most popular floral accessory for brides and their attendants. The choice of flowers and headdress will be influenced by how the bride will be wearing her hair and whether or not she chooses to wear a veil. It should be planned to tie in with the bridal bouquet.

materials

a head of *Hydrangea macrophylla* 'Mein Liebling'
a stem of *Helleborus orientalis*
2 stems of everlasting sweet pea (*Lathyrus latifolius* 'Albus')
2 stems of flowering *Eucalyptus perriniana*
5 stems of *Rosa* 'Mimi Eden'
a selection of silver wires
a roll of green Parafilm
a selection of fine wires – 0.28mm and 0.32mm
a firm plastic headband

step by step

1 The size, shape, and structure of the flowers and foliage will determine which wiring technique is required. As long as the method works and the wire gauge is correct for the purpose and all the visible wires are concealed, it does not really matter how this has been achieved. The eucalyptus leaves used in this headdress have been wired with a double leg mount. To create one, take a silver wire, make a hairpin bend, and fold one wire over the other three times. The same method has been used for the flowering eucalyptus. The everlasting sweet pea and hydrangea have been wired by taking a few flowerets and placing a wire through the fleshy part of the stem and then looping one wire over the other three times. The rose and the hellebores have been wired by placing a wire through the base of the flower head. To do this, put a silver wire into the calyx, carefully twist around the base of the calyx, and then bring it down the stem, looping one wire over the other three times in all.

2 When you have wired all the flower heads, flowerets and leaves, tape them with floral tape.

3 Take the plastic headband and cover it with the Parafilm. This will make it easier to tape on your wires, and it also gives the headband a natural green color. Starting with the eucalyptus leaf at the end, bind individual flowers to the plastic headband by stretching the Parafilm. Alternate each flower, working across each side of the headband and edging with the leaves. Continue all the way across until you have reached the other side.

All-round floral headdresses or circlets are made by creating a round floral frame by overlapping two 0.71mm wires and overlapping them with another two 0.71mm wires, binding them together with 0.20mm silver wire and then creating a round circlet with two hooks to fit the size desired. Individual wired and gutted flower heads are then taped onto the frame in the same way as for a headband.

LEFT A round wreath to be worn on the crown of the head has been made from variegated ivy leaves, flowerets of tuberosa, pink ranunculus, and muscari.

seasonal wreath

materials

a 14-inch wire wreath frame
a bag of sphagnum moss
a bunch of Ivy berries (*Hedera helix*)
a bunch of blue pine (*Pinus wallichiana*)
a bunch of Scots pine (*Pinus sylvestris*)
a bunch of *Skimmia japonica* 'Rubinetta"
a bunch of holly berries (*Ilex aquifolium* 'Madam Briot')
a length of silver ribbon
a spool of silver cord
a pair of scissors
a reel of florist's wire (0.56mm)
one 0.90mm stub wire

Throughout the world, rings and wreaths of fresh or dried plant materials have traditionally been used as a symbol of eternity and hospitality, and this remains a significant gesture today. Wreaths that are used to decorate a door are constructed on a mossed base, which is a better foundation than floral foam. Foam only works for flower heads and for temporary or short celebrations. To most wreaths, heavy decorations and embellishments such as cones and fruits are added, which need to be well anchored into the moss to survive the festive period.

OPPOSITE A large open floral foam heart frame has been edged with ivy trails wired into the base and then topped with a mass of multicolored roses. Trails of ivy and muehlenbeckia vines have been added on top of the flowers to give a more natural feel. Wired paper butterflies have been wired into the design.

step by step

1 Wind the end of the spool of wire onto the inner frame of the wreath ring. Meanwhile tease apart the sphagnum moss, removing any branches, leaves, cones, or other foreign bodies. Place several handfuls of moss about two inches high on the frame and bind the moss on firmly. Continue adding moss evenly and binding diagonally across the frame until it is completely covered with moss. Once completed, bind the spool wire around the frame for a second time and make sure the density of the moss is even throughout. Cut the wire and place the end into the moss and, with a pair of floristry scissors, trim off any straggly pieces of moss.

2 Attach the spool wire again to the edge of the frame and then start to bind on bunches of cut foliage about 1½ to 2 inches long. To create a good binding, trim the lower stem

of additional foliage. Carry on around the ring in an counter-clockwise fashion using groups of foliage.

3 Repeat the pattern of foliage until you have created a lovely variegated ring that has lots of different textures as well as colors within it.

4 When you have completed the ring, push a pair of scissors through the back of the frame and ease in the cord to attach the wreath to a doorway.

5 Create three loops of ribbon and wire through the center with a 0.90mm wire and then pin into the base of the frame.

topiary candelabra

Every decorating florist needs a good set of sturdy metal table candelabras that can be dressed up for any season or event. I love the effect of covering the metal stems and arms with plant material so that the candelabra become more of a topiary form than a candelabra. Hebe, rosemary, ivy, box, and eucalyptus are among my favorites, and in the wintertime, I love to use dogwood, berried cotoneaster, contorted willow, and spruce. For spring, pussy willow and blossom are effective, as well as catkin-laden birch. For any season, equisetum works well, as does this painted birch, which I buy dipped in paint, but you could spray paint if you do not have access to supplies of painted birch.

materials

a metal 5-prong candelabra
a 20-inch floral foam wreath
2 bunches of painted birch twigs
a spool of heavy blue wire
5 taper candles
a block of floral foam
a roll of pot tape
Floraltac adhesive
5 stems of hydrangea
15 stems of *Eustoma russellium*
'Fuji Silver Blue'
7 stems of *Agapanthus*
'Atlantic Ocean'
32 stems of *Rosa* 'Sterling Silver'
10 stems of stock (*Mathiola incana*
'Centum Lavender')
a bunch of *Senecio greyii*
a bunch of berried ivy *Hedera helix*
a bunch of *Hebe albicans* 'Red Edge'

step by step

1 Bind the stem of the candlestick with the birch twigs using the spool wire. Place the soaked floral foam in the center of the candlestick and tape it into place. Soak the floral ring and stand around the base of the candlestick. Trim off the edge of the foam to make it easier to add the plant material. Paring a little off the edge and smoothing the shape is sometimes referred to as chamfering.

2 Place the ivy in the floral foam, working from all angles to create a loose shape, including some trails down the candlestick. Fill in with senecio and hebe to give a good outline and shape. Fill the ring with foliage all around so that you cover the floral foam ring.

3 Starting with the largest flowers, position the hydrangea flower heads around the candelabra. For the top arrangement you should be aiming for a ball shape. Continue to build the shape with the agapanthus, stocks, and lisianthus. Finally place your roses in pairs throughout the arrangement. Repeat the process with the remaining flowers to fill up the floral foam ring at the base of the arrangement.

4 Finally place your roses in pairs throughout the arrangement and complete by placing the candles. Secure the base of the candles in the candelabra with floral tac.

RIGHT A single-stemmed candelabra has been covered with hebe with bind wire, and 'Avalanche' roses and cream 'Gracia' spray roses have been wired and placed into the greenery.

wired fruit basket

Using fruits and vegetables has been a trademark of my designs for two decades. I often get inspiration from the fruit and vegetable market with all the lovely textures and colors of the produce, particularly when flowers are more expensive and scarce in the fall and winter time. This basket arrangement has been perennially popular either in the summer with green apples and pastel summer flowers, or in the fall and winter with red apples and dramatic color combinations.

materials

a strong sturdy basket
a plastic bowl
4 blocks of green floral foam
a roll of pot tape
0.90 mm Floral wire
30 red apples
a bunch of sphagnum moss
5 stems of American oak (*Quercus palustris*)
a bunch of ivy berries (*Hedera helix*)
10 stems of red *Skimmia japonica* 'Rubella'
5 stems of golden holly berries (*Ilex aquifolium* 'Golden Verboom')
10 stems of *Rudbeckia hirta*
7 stems of *Leucospermum cordiolium* 'Succession'
15 stems of *Rosa* 'Ruby Red'
15 stems of *Rosa* 'Acqua'

step by step

1 Wire the thirty apples by pushing an 0.90mm florist wire through the lower half of the fruit so that an equal amount protrudes from each side. Then place a second wire in the other direction of the lower part of the fruit and then twist all four wires together leaving two wire stems which can be used to attach the apple to the basket frame.

2 Starting with the bottom layer attach fifteen apples around the edge of the basket. When you have completed the bottom tier, wire the second layer into the basket frame.

3 Then fill a large plastic liner with four blocks of soaked floral foam. Secure in the liner with pot tape and then fit snugly into the basket by placing sphagnum moss all around. Make sure that the floral foam is at least two inches above the edge of the container so you can create a rounded effect.

4 Starting with the ivy berries, trim into branches of about three inches and place all around the basket at different heights, but all radiating from a central point. Then follow with the skimmia and American oak until you can hardly see the floral foam. By now you should have created a lovely rounded structure into which you can put your flowers.

5 First cut the ilex berries into branches of three to four inches and place these around the arrangement, and then add the leucospermums and the textural rudbeckia. Finally add the roses in groups of threes.

conical topiary

Conical or geometric-shaped arrangements are usually created for celebrations. By using chicken wire and moss, you can construct much larger arrangements with more densely packed flowers than you can using floral foam. It also allows you to create any size of arrangement you wish. For a corporate event in an enormous atrium, we have made arrangements as large as twenty feet tall. The larger the topiary required, the more sophisticated the structure or mechanics have to be.

materials

a metal urn
a conical topiary frame
½ yard of chicken wire
a bale of sphagnum moss
a spool of heavy
florist wire
5 bunches of *Narcissi
tazetta* 'Laurens Koster'
5 bunches of orange
Ranuculus 'Ranobelle
Inra Zalm'
50 stems of yellow
Calendula officianalis
'Greenheart Orange'
50 stems of *Rosa*
'Lemonade'
50 stems of *Rosa* 'Milva'
10 stems of *Forsythia
intermedia* 'Spectabilis'
2 bunches of *Camellia
japonica*
30 sharon fruit
30 stems of
*Leucospermum
cordifolium* 'Fireball'

step by step

1 Line the cone in chicken wire and then stuff it with sphagnum moss so that it is very firm.

2 Using the spool wire, bind the chicken wire onto the frame and then wire it into the iron urn so that it is very stable.

3 Cover the frame with small sprigs of camellia foliage placed in the moss. Then arrange the ten stems of forsythia in the bottom of the urn and place vertically around the frame so that they all meet at the top. Secure them with hairpin bends of heavy stub wire.

4 Next prepare all your flowers. Wire them by placing a heavy stub wire up the stem and into the flower head. Place two wires through the sharon fruit and then twist them together at the base.

5 Place the sharon fruit in the moss, evenly spaced. Add all the wired flowers, placing the narcissi last as they are the most delicate.

part three

celebrations

One of the greatest joys of working as a florist is that you get the chance to create beautiful flowers for all the occasions that mark one's life. Mostly, these are celebratory, and even when they sadly mark a death or are for remembrance, the sentiment expressed through the flowers is to celebrate life. Flowers lighten our senses and enhance any event. Whichever floral decorations you choose and however you achieve your design, your flowers will be central to the occasion and will symbolize the hope and love of your celebrations.

decorating your space

The choice of flowers, hardware, and scale will all be determined by the space that you have to decorate and of course the budget. It is the skill of a good florist to make the most of the flowers whatever the budget so that they really get noticed and have the greatest impact. The type of occasion and event will also determine the choice.

In domestic situations, there is normally one favorite place or several areas where you like to display your flowers. Most people select their flowers on the criteria of their space or their favorite vases. They have areas in their homes that have the most impact and choose their flowers on that basis.

For a large cocktail party where everyone will mainly be standing, a large, tall central arrangement will be more visible than lots of smaller vases. If the hall is very big as well as tall, I often use a number of 3-feet-high vases on occasional tables filled with orchids and tall papyrus to spread the color and flowers throughout the party. A grand hall will also demand a more dramatic tall display where either large pedestals or topiary forms will be needed to suit

the scale. In a cathedral, two large urns and plinths on either side of the altar make more visual impact than decorating lots of pew ends.

The larger the venue, the more hardware you will need, and possibly greater planning since you may need to bring in equipment to make your creations, such as ladders and cherry pickers, and larger vans to transport the frames, mechanics, and the hardware as well as the flowers. Working onsite like this also requires public liability insurance, and many venues and banquet halls have specific rules and contracts governing who can work on their events. Always check first with the banqueting manager and take as much protection in the form of drop cloths and plastic liners and make sure you have all the materials you need for cleaning up after you have finished you work. It is also important to talk to the banqueting coordinator or wedding planner so you are given an appropriate time to arrive so you can dress the clothed tables. It is advisable to be at the venue before the lighting engineers since they will be enhancing your displays once

LEFT Three vases have been filled with anthurium heads suspended by gold aluminum wire. It is best to build this up from the bottom of the vase to the top and then fill with water to keep the flowers from floating to the top. The aluminum wire holds them in place when water is added. They last up to a week before becoming transparent.

OPPOSITE LEFT Asymmetrical arrangements grouped together have been popular now for a few years. Here again, part of the interest lies in having oversized vases and then filling them with aluminum wire to keep the flowers in place. The long-stemmed calla lilies have been bunched with swirls of wires to keep the flower heads in place. The effect makes a strong impact.

they are in place and all the tables are dressed. Floral designers sometimes work as party planners and select the other contractors they work with and are responsible for the whole design. More often they liase with party planners and caterers, each adding their expertise to make the event truly special.

For traditional and country venues, wilder and more classical styles of arrangements work better than minimal, geometric designs. A stark, modern venue may be perfect for the current vogue of minimal displays, but it rarely works well if the scale of building is too vast, because these type of arrangements get lost. Often this style of arranging is minimal on flowers but very heavy on hardware, requiring expensive, large vases and plinths, not to mention very good lighting. Glass vases with suspended flowers look fantastic if lit up, and you get a lot of impact with not very many flowers so this is very economical on perishable products.

Whatever style you work in, every florist needs to have a good selection of hardware to create well-balanced, creative floral displays, and very often for the event florist, it soon means you have a warehouse of accoutrements for flower arranging so that you can work in any style of building and for any kind of event!

There are so many ways to decorate a space, which is why there are so many different techniques to learn. Arches are great for church doorways for wedding ceremonies, and they also provide the perfect canopy under which the bride and groom can be married. Depending on whether they are freestanding or placed against a wall will determine what kind of mechanics you require and how it may be constructed. Some churches have perfect pews for decorating while others have replaced their original pews or are modern and have chairs that do not suit floral decorations so easily. For a traditional christening, the emphasis will be on decorating the front area of a church.

Tents literally offer a blank canvas and are among my favorite to decorate. They are large spaces, but can be inexpensively decorated by hiring topiary from garden nurseries and by adding just one or two really stunning displays. For any large venue, I prefer to use low table decorations to spread the color throughout the space.

Finally, using seasonal flowers will always be the best way of making use of a budget, and it is always a good idea to bear in mind the budget and the scale when ordering your flowers. The directory section on pages 186 to189 will help you make your selections.

One long flower trough makes a perfect container for a large flower display such as this. I have a set of long baskets with zinc liners, but I often use a terra-cotta flower trough with a plastic liner and fill it with upright blocks of floral foam to give me lots of area to place a lot of front-facing and downward-proportioned plant material. For this early summer mantelpiece arrangement, I have chosen gerberas, *viburnum opulous*, euphorbia fulgens, cymbidium orchids, leucospermum, and 'calmia,' 'Beauty by Oger,' and 'Luxor' roses mixed with trailing ivies, solomon's seal, and white leaf foliages.

OPPOSITE For my own home at Christmas, I often choose to use spray trays filled with foam and decorate two sides of the mantelpiece just using variegated foliages and a few thick altar candles. It is amazing how long a simple foliage arrangement lasts. Ivy, holly, photinia, and senecio look very festive with just a few wired ribbon bows. The suspended wreath is made from dried pomegranates glued onto a straw frame. The arrangements shown here are classical designs, but you can just as easily create a more contemporary look by placing groups of vases with candles or votives.

Mantelpieces are great locations for flower arrangements because they place the flowers at eye level and give a spectacular display, taking up very little room.

LEFT A birthday cake arrangement designed on a round posy pad of foam. The base has been covered with asparagus fern and camellia, and the lime-green balls are *Asclepias* 'Moby Dick.' The main flowers are pink ranunculus and 'Cherry Brandy' roses. The soft pink starry astrantia brings the taper candle color through the arrangement.

The summer months are a great time for using bright colors as the light levels are higher and it suits the mood. The use of color is very connected to the seasons, and while hot climates such as India and Mexico are crazy about color, I had not discerned any link with food until, during a long discussion with my German friend and master florist Gregor Lersch, he observed that our taste in floristry is not so dissimilar to our native diet. Northern European food is more bland than the spicy cuisines of South America and Asia. In Northern Europe, paler colors are more prevalent with an emphasis on neutrals. To this day, I would say that the refined English taste is still to choose all white in the home, as it is deemed tasteful. I doubt very much that an Asian or South American would see the value of white in the same way!

ABOVE 'Cherry Brandy,' 'Jade,' and 'Aqua' roses have been hand tied with lime-green 'Revert' chrysanthemums and orange leucospermum in the lime, orange, and pink color mix. Orange kumquats conceal the stems in a cube vase.

LEFT The swirls of the fabric have been continued through this design, using roses and kumquats, which have been threaded onto a heavy florist wire. The muehlenbeckia vine adds a natural touch to the vibrancy of the flowers.

OPPOSITE The colors of the table runner have been mirrored in the flower designs and tableware. Three square dishes contain brightly colored roses and kumquats. Deep red vanda orchids are dotted along the muehlenbeckia vine.

Outdoor parties require flowers that are natural and wild, and suit the environment in which they are going to be seen. Ideally, garden parties should reflect the planting in the garden, and therefore require a more mixed composition. Seasonal flowers are usually my choice; in springtime I use bulb or tuber flowers such as tulips or ranunculus; later in the year I go for blossom, lilacs, and early peonies, and in summertime I love to use lavender, garden roses, and sweet peas. For late summer, I opt for the richer palettes of dark red dahlias, bright golden sunflowers, and tall lilies.

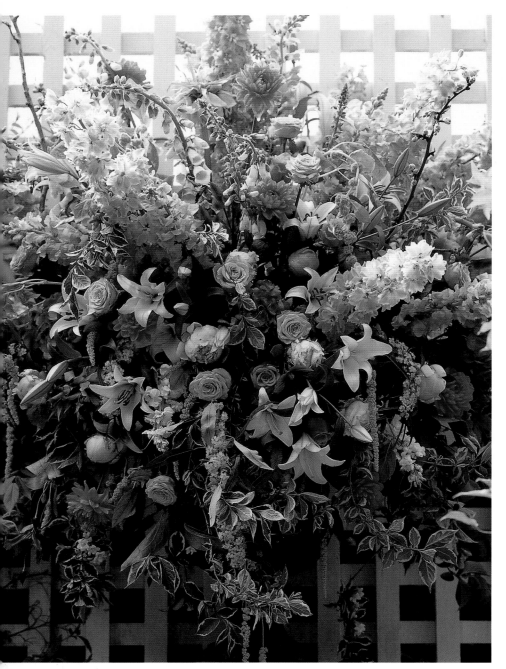

ABOVE Pinks, oranges, and lilacs have been made more vibrant with the use of alchemilla mollis and the textual gray foliage senecio greyii. Low flower arrangements allow you to talk across the table, and I always like to choose some flowers that are scented when arranging flowers in the garden. Sweet peas are one of my favorite flowers to grow in my garden and are often used in my work.

LEFT Here in my own garden I have selected the flowers to tone with my fabrics on the table and seat pads. The selection of linen is a key role of the florist because it provides an important backdrop for your floral designs.

OPPOSITE For the table I have used two long spray trays surrounded by brightly colored silk lanterns. The two garden chairs have been sculptured out of metal and birch. An external pedestal arrangement is used as a focal point beyond the floral arch. This draws the eye beyond the table. Paper butterflies have been used throughout the garden, adding a colorful and delicate touch to the whole *al fresco* ensemble.

OPPOSITE A buffet table is set for a celebratory afternoon tea. Foam rings around storm lanterns make perfect centerpieces for an informal table setting. As these decorative elements are large, I have chosen to use large-headed flowers, such as the white dill, pink lilies, and peonies. A floral cake decoration has been designed using smaller-headed flowers, such as pink ranunculus and astrantia.

TOP LEFT The growth in lifestyle accessories has led to a huge increase in the accoutrements to the floral trade. Bright pink hanging votives add some color to an ancient apple tree.

TOP RIGHT Scented lilies nestle among some white dill. Certain scents bring back memories, and I love the musky scent of lilies because it reminds me of my own wedding day!

MIDDLE LEFT A napkin is tied with organza bows and paper butterflies.

MIDDLE RIGHT Fashions come and go, but pink remains a favorite, and ranunculus are my very favorite flowers.

BOTTOM LEFT The dill gives these other showy flowers, such as lilies and dahlias, a more country feel.

BOTTOM RIGHT Floral cake decorations are easy to make. I usually use a small piece of floral foam in the cut-off base of a white styrofoam cup. This one is filled with flowering weigelia, ranunculus, roses, and astrantia.

Long tables often require a series of vases down the center. When entertaining at home I prefer to have several vases in a repeated sequence along the table so that I also have room for large plates and servers. With several vases, the eye moves along the table, and the flowers should be high enough to give a good floral presence, but not so high that the guests cannot see one another. There are many vases available now that are around six to eight inches high, which is perfect for a table center. The most popular color schemes are still white and green with a touch of color, and the color schemes on these pages continue to be classic favorites each year, whatever the current floral vogue is.

OPPOSITE Pale pink peonies, dahlias, and sweet peas have been mixed with *Alchemilla mollis*, hydrangea, and vines of clematis montana. The frosted pink vases are perfectly toned for the flowers and the table runner.

ABOVE Napkin flowers are a lovely way of bringing the color of the flowers across the table. Here forget-me-nots, hellebores, and early blossom make a very pretty spring touch to the table.

LEFT One way of keeping a lovely napkin posy alive is to arrange the flowers in a plastic vial of water, covered with a leaf tied with raffia. Here blossom, catkins, ranunculus, hellebores, and eryngium are all able to stay fresh. At the end of the meal, guests may like to have the individual posy as a keepsake to remind them of the occasion.

ABOVE I have always loved to use leeks in my arrangements because Ilove the graduation of color from the roots on the bottom to the lush green stems of the vegetables. Baby leeks have been placed around a small glass cylinder and then filled with a hand-tied bouquet of *Viburnum opulous*, alchemilla mollis, white peonies, and 'Renate' roses.

ABOVE LEFT A posy of hand-tied gypsophila and 'Vendelle' roses. The soft-colored 'Vendelle' rose tends to go very well with ivory fabric, which is often chosen by brides in preference to white because it is more flattering.

ABOVE MIDDLE Some flower heads are so beautiful they are best admired on their own. These eucharis lilies are a very pure white with lovely lime-green centers.

ABOVE RIGHT Hydrangea, peonies, and gypsophila arranged in their own frosted vases.

MIDDLE LEFT Beautiful, polished shells add to the glamour of the day and embellish the table decorations. Small shells have been cut to hold placecards.

LEFT Delicate eucharist lilies and gypsophila in frosted vases provide a sumptuous display.

I love to use several different heights and shapes of vases made in the same material. Here frosted vases of different heights have been used to decorate an ivory and gold wedding table. The simple use of several different vases of all one type of flower gives a sumptuous look. The peony chair backs are tied with organza ribbon and on the side table there are vases of white flocked sumata twigs, white massed hydrangea, and white everlasting sweet pea. A floral lei of Singapore orchids links with a trio of tall frosted vases.

flower directory

The flower trade is so international and on such a huge global scale of production that seasonality of flowers is no longer such an important issue for the floral designer. However, I have to say that flowers that are still only available in their season and are therefore slightly rarer are the ones I treasure, more than ones I can buy any week of the year. Below is a list of some of our most used and favorite seasonal flowers and foliages by their most commonly known name in the flower trade.

early spring

1 Tulip
2 Anemone
3 Ranunculus
4 Hyacinth
5 Hellebore
6 Ivy
7 Lilac
8 Snowdrop
9 Daffodil
10 Hippeastrum (also called amaryllis)
11 Almond blossom
12 Cherry blossom
13 Myrtle
14 Magnolia
15 Skimmia
16 Snowberry
17 Flame euphorbia
18 Freesia
19 Forsythia
20 Pussy willow

mid spring

1 Narcissus
2 Forget-me-not
3 Grape hyacinth
4 Hyaciinth
5 Iris
6 Violet
7 Arum lily (also called calla lily)
8 Poppy
9 Mimosa
10 Fosythia
11 Catkin
12 Pussy willow
13 Tuberose
14 Ranunculus
15 Crown Imperial
16 Hellebore
17 Tulip
18 Prunus
19 Solomon's seal
20 Camellia

late spring

1 Guelder rose
2 Lilac
3 Bluebell
4 Lily-of-the-Valley
5 Freesia
6 Campanula
7 Wallflower
8 Sweet pea
9 Ranunculus
10 Euphorbia
11 Snake's head fritillary
12 Broom
13 Moluccella
14 Red hot poker
15 Iris
16 Ixia
17 Tulip
18 Godetia
19 Spiraea
20 Trollius

FROM TOP LEFT:
Hyacinthus orientalis 'Delt Blue'/white *Muscari* and *Narcissus tazetta* 'Avalanche'/*Tulipa* 'Gander Rhapsody' and *Tulipa* 'Synaeda Blue'

early summer

1 Peony
2 Sweet pea
3 Alchemilla
4 Scabious
5 Solomon's seal
6 Hosta leaves
7 Allium
8 Lisianthus
9 Astilbe
10 Cornflower
11 Rose
12 Aquilegia
13 Margeurite daisy
14 Sweet william
15 Gardenia
16 Stephanotis
17 Jasmine
18 Dill
19 Brodiaea
20 Lavender

mid summer

1 Astrantia
2 Delphinium
3 Agapanthus
4 Angelica
5 Artichoke
6 Flowering mint
7 Poppy
8 Nerine
9 Lupin
10 Larkspur
11 Foxglove
12 Snapdragon
13 Foxtail lily
14 Celosia
15 Zinnia
16 Hollyhock
17 Stock
18 Tuberose
19 Clematis
20 Phlox

late summer

1 Love-in-a-mist
2 Dahlia
3 Veronica
4 Monkshood
5 Marjoram
6 Bouvardia
7 Sunflower
8 Hydrangea
9 Sage
10 Gladioli
11 Sedum
12 Chocolate cosmos
13 Blackberry
14 Fountain grass
15 Aquilegia
16 Tracelium
17 Thistle
18 Ageratum
19 Old man's beard
20 Hebe

FROM TOP RIGHT:
Paeonia lactiflora 'Karl Rosenfield'/*Rosa* 'Grand Prix,' *Rosa* 'Milano,' *Rosa* 'Acqua'/*Dahlia* 'Arabian Night'

early fall

1 Amaranthus
2 Cotinus
3 Snowberry
4 Bullrush
5 Blackberry
6 Dahlia
7 Curcuma
8 Belladonna lily
9 Scabious seed heads
10 Allium
11 Rudbeckia
12 Dill
13 Lipstick reed
14 Millet
15 Bupleurum
16 Asclepias
17 Aster
18 Pistachio
19 Chinese lantern
20 Miscanthus

mid fall

1 Chili
2 Crab apple
3 Hypericum
4 Blackberry
5 Leucospermum
6 Arum lily (also called calla lily)
7 Chrysanthemum
8 Photinia
9 Lotus seed heads
10 American oak leaves
11 Beech
12 Callicarpa
13 Gourd
14 Cotinus
15 Red hot poker
16 Asclepias
17 Sunflower
18 Dogwood stems
19 Hypericum
20 Rattlesnake ginger

late fall

1 Ornamental cabbage
2 Kangaroo paw
3 Crab apple
4 Leucodendron
5 Gourd
6 Chinese lantern
7 Holly berries
8 Hop
9 Flame euphorbia
10 Solidago
11 Rudbeckia
12 Shampoo ginger
13 Chincherinchee
14 Helconia
15 Hanging helconia
16 Water lily
17 Nerine
18 Limonium
19 Ligustrum berries
20 Amaranthus

FROM TOP LEFT:
Helianthus annus
'Flame'/*Ilex aquilfolium*
'GoldenVerboon'/
Crysanthemum
'Tom Pearce'

early winter

1 Globe thistle
2 Helconia
3 Witch hazel
4 Protea
5 Bird of paradise
6 Queen protea
7 King protea
8 Galax leaves
9 Trachelium
10 Dogwood stems
11 Chrysanthemum
12 Skimmia
13 Grevillea
14 Ginger lily
15 Ornamental pineapple
16 Craspedia
17 Cotoneaster berries
18 Ligustrum berries
19 Crab apples
20 Lichen branches'

mid winter

1 Photinia
2 Mistletoe
3 Tulip
4 Vanda orchid
5 Hippeastrum (also called amaryllis)
6 Eucalyptus seed pods
7 Ivy
8 Blue pine
9 Willow
10 Hypericum
11 Blueberry
12 Cymbidium orchid
13 Dendrobium orchid
14 Holly
15 Holly berries
16 Box
17 Anthurium
18 Pinus stobus
19 Oncidium orchid'
20 Mahonia

late winter

1 Peace lily
2 Snowflake
3 Brunia
4 Hippeastrum (also called amaryllis)
5 Carthamus
6 Arum lily (also called calla lily)
7 Broom
8 Heather
9 Silver kochia
10 Tulip
11 Anemone
12 Ranunculus
13 Brassica
14 Phalenopsis orchid
15 Slipper orchid
16 Banksia
17 Hibiscus
18 Cotton
19 Larch
20 Laurel

FROM TOP RIGHT:
Hippastrum 'Mont
Blanc'/*Helleborus orientalis*
'Trotter's Spotted'/
Leucojum 'Spring
Snowflake'

index

acknowledgments

To produce any illustrated book, there is a large team who work together very hard, and often over a long period of time to achieve the end result. This stunning book has been no exception, and I have had the privilege to work with many dedicated people who were prepared to contribute their many talents (and go that extra mile) to make this book so special, and who have also been great fun to work with. It was my great pleasure to work with Sian Irvine who has produced all the stunning photography. These wonderful images have enhanced my work, and have been beautifully designed in this book by the Art Director Maggie Town. I like to have a little flexibility on what I may produce each shoot day, depending on what inspires me at the flower market, and this can start to be a little of a headache, and just enormously annoying when you are trying to lay out a book. Maggie has been amazingly tolerant, and done a really wonderful job! As usual, I have a long suffering Editor who has had to cajole, coax, and encourage some text out of me, and I am particularly grateful to Kate John for her sympathetic yet firm approach.

Over the years I have had the pleasure to work with some very talented florists, and at present I have a very special staff, many of which have been with me a long time. Sarah Jackson has been brilliant in cheerfully organising the day-to-day running of my business, and has contributed enormously to the creativity of this book, along with Rachel Mashiter, Samantha Griffiths, and Anita Everard, who work on special events, weddings, and at The Flower School. To the rest of the Paula Pryke Flower team based at The Flower House: Ann, Tania, Gina, Jo, Anne, Penny and Jis Sook, thank you; Chris and Anna, thank you for doing such a wonderful job at Liberty with Hisako, Monica, Mira and Angela; Anita and Natasha, and all the great team outside The Conran Shop at Brompton Cross, thank you. Thanks also to all my fantastic (long standing and long suffering) suppliers, particularly Dennis Edwards, Marcel Van Eijsden, and Kees Ross who supply the lovely flowers and have supported and encouraged me enormously in my flower enterprises.

And thanks to all my clients!

For details of the Paula Pryke Flower School, please contact:
The Flower School, Cynthia Street, London N1 9JF, UNITED KINGDOM.
Tel: (44) 20 77837 7373   Website: www.paula-pryke-flowers.com